D1413627

Student Edition

Cadenza the Cat™, Bebop the Cat™, Gusto the Bulldog™, Largo the Snail™, P.F. (Piano Forte)™, Octavia™, and Maestro™
are trademarks of Warner Bros. Publications. All Rights Reserved.

Expressions Music Curriculum™, Music Expressions™, Band Expressions™, Jazz Expressions™,
Orchestra Expressions™, Choral Expressions™, Piano Expressions™, and Guitar Expressions™
are trademarks of Warner Bros. Publications. All Rights Reserved.

1 2 3 4 5 6 7 8 9 10   08 07 06 05 04 03

© 2003 WARNER BROS. PUBLICATIONS U.S. INC.
All Rights Reserved

Any duplication, adaptation or arrangement of the compositions
contained in this publication requires the consent of the Publisher.
No part of this publication may be photocopied or reproduced in any way without permission.
Unauthorized uses are an infringement of the U.S. Copyright Act and are punishable thereunder.

Warner Bros. Publications • 15800 NW 48th Avenue • Miami, FL 33014

COMPLETE TEACHER EDITION (EMC3001)
UPC: 6-54979-05763-5
ISBN: 0-7579-1183-8 90000

TEACHER EDITION, VOLUME I (EMC3001A)
UPC: 6-54979-05767-3
ISBN: 0-7579-1187-0 90000

TEACHER EDITION, VOLUME II (EMC3001B)
UPC: 6-54979-05766-6
ISBN: 0-7579-1186-2 90000

TEACHER EDITION, VOLUME III (EMC3001C)
UPC: 6-54979-05765-9
ISBN: 0-7579-1185-4 90000

TEACHER EDITION, VOLUME IV (EMC3001D)
UPC: 6-54979-05764-2
ISBN: 0-7579-1184-6 90000

STUDENT EDITION (EMC3002)
UPC: 6-54979-05760-4
ISBN: 0-7579-1182-X 90000

Credits

PROJECT CREATORS & COORDINATORS

Robert W. Smith

Susan L. Smith

PROJECT EDITOR

Judith M. Stoehr

AUTHORS

Judith M. Stoehr
Lead Author
Creative Insights
Omaha, Nebraska

June M. Hinckley
Department of Education
Tallahassee, Florida

Darla S. Hanley, Ph.D.
Shenandoah University
Winchester, Virginia

Carolyn C. Minear
Orange County Public Schools
Orlando, Florida

CONTRIBUTING AUTHORS

Timothy S. Brophy, Ph.D.
Assessment Specialist
University of Florida
Gainesville, Florida

Art Williams
Media Specialist
Troy, Alabama

CONSULTANTS

June M. Hinckley
National Standards for the Arts Consultant
Department of Education
Tallahassee, Florida

James Clarke
Fine Art Consultant
Executive Director
Texas Coalition for Quality Arts Education
Houston, Texas

Kathy Robinson
Multicultural Consultant
Eastman School of Music
Rochester, New York

David Peters
Technology Coordinator
University of Indiana
Indianapolis, Indiana

Doug Brasell
Website Coordinator
Cairo, Georgia

Artie Almeida
Listening Maps
Bear Lake Elementary School
Apopka, Florida

MULTICULTURAL AMBASSADORS & CONTRIBUTORS

Toshio Akayama
Professor Emeritus
Musashino School of Music
Tokyo, Japan

Kathy Robinson
Eastman School of Music
Rochester, New York

ORCHESTRA

Michael L. Alexander
Houston, Texas

Gerald E. Anderson
Los Angeles, California

Kathleen DeBerry Brungard
Charlotte, North Carolina

Sandra Dackow
Trenton, New Jersey

Anne C. Witt
Arlington, Texas

BAND

Jim Campbell
Lexington, Kentucky

Richard C. Crain
The Woodlands, Texas

Linda Gammon
Fairfax, Virginia

Gary Markham
Atlanta, Georgia

Michael Story
Houston, Texas

JAZZ

J. Richard Dunscomb
Atlanta, Georgia

Jose Diaz
Houston, Texas

Dr. Willie L. Hill, Jr.
Amherst, Massachusetts

Jerry Tolson
Louisville, Kentucky

CHORAL

Dr. Darla S. Hanley
Winchester, Virginia

Jim Kimmell
Nashville, Tennessee

Dr. Russ Robinson
Gainesville, Florida

Jerry Tolson
Louisville, Kentucky

CONTRIBUTORS

Pilot and Practicing Teachers:

Kara Bell, *Great Falls, MT*

Cheryl Black, *Camden, SC*

W. Elaine Blocher, *Derby, KS*

Karen Bouton, *Graceville, FL*

Patty Brennan, *Chesapeake, VA*

Temetia Creed, *Tampa, FL*

Scott T. Evans, *Orlando, FL*

Debbie Fahmie, *Kissimmee, FL*

David Fox, *Oviedo, FL*

Mary Gibson, *Maitland, FL*

Claudette Gray, *Pittsburgh, PA*

Lisa Hamer, *Moncks Corner, SC*

Julie Harmon, *North Platte, NE*

Jennifer Hartman, *Shawnee, KS*

Elaine Hashem, *Penacook, NH*

Mark Hodges, *Sumter, SC*

Beverly Holl, *Los Angeles, CA*

Grace Jordan, *Orlando, FL*

Lyn Koch, *Pittsburgh, PA*

Eunice Marrero, *Orlando, FL*

Nancy McBride, *Anderson, SC*

Kathleen Scott Meske,
Los Angeles, CA

Deborah Mosier, *Bennington, NE*

Debi Noel, *Eugene, OR*

Keisha C. Pendergrass,
Clover, SC

Teresa Sims, *Troy, AL*

Marjorie Smith, *Lutz, FL*

Lisa Stern, *Winter Park, FL*

Julie A. Swank, *Troy, OH*

Jane Wall, *Wexford, PA*

Kirsten H. Wilcox,
Winchester, VA

Leslie A. Wooten, *LaGrange, KY*

RECORDING

Robert Dingley
Executive Producer

Robert W. Smith
Producer

Jack Lamb
Associate Producer

Kendall Thomsen
Recording Engineer

Andy de Ganahl
Mix Engineer

Jason May
Mix Engineer

MUSIC ARRANGING

Robert W. Smith

Michael Story

Jack Bullock

Victor Lopez

Timothy S. Brophy

Don Beattie
Piano Accompaniments

Delayna Beattie
Piano Accompaniments

WARNER BROS. PUBLICATIONS

Fred Anton
CEO

Robert Dingley
Vice President: Education

David Hakim
Vice President: Sales

Andrea Nelson
Vice President: Marketing

Lourdes Carreras-Balepogi
Marketing Coordinator

David Olsen
Director: Business Affairs

PRODUCTION

Thom Proctor
Project Manager

Gayle Giese
Production Editor

Bill Galliford
Music Arranging Assistance

Donna Wheeler
Editorial Assistance

Heather Mahone
Editorial Assistance

Susan Buckey
Editorial Assistance

Dr. Arlene Sukraw
Editorial Assistance

Nadine DeMarco
Text Proofreader

Nancy Rehm
Senior Art Director

Shawn Martinez
Assistant Art Director

Thais Yanes
Student Book Page Layout

Al Nigro
Music Engraving Manager

Mark Young
Music Engraver

Glenda Mikell
Music Engraver

Glyn Dryhurst
Director, Production Services

Hank Fields
Production Coordinator

Sharon Marlow
Production Assistance

TEACHER EDITION INTERIOR LAYOUT

InterMedia
A Mad 4 Marketing Company

Margaret Stapleton
Project Director

Anne Rogers
Production Coordinator

Marie LaFauci
Senior Artist

Maureen Hyman

Leo Jones

Dana Kaufman

Roque Rodón

Linda Smith

Elyse Taylor

Michelle M. White

Amy Wertzler

ACKNOWLEDGMENTS
Thanks to:

Ottmar Liebert, for permission to use the photo on page 42 (photo credit: Reisig & Taylor).

Sweet Honey in the Rock (www.sweethoney.com), for permission to use their photo on page 58 (photo © Dwight Carter).

Michael Lutch, for the photos of the Boston Pops on page 78 (© Michael Lutch).

"The President's Own" United States Marine Band, for the courtesy of providing the concert band photo on pages 94–95.

Hohner, Inc./HSS, for the courtesy of providing photos of Sonor Orff instruments on pages 206–207.

Elizabeth Dworkin, Dworkin/Eliason Partners, for permission to use the photo of Cynthia Phelps on page 222 (photo credit: J. Henry Fair).

Minoru Miki, for permission to use his photo on page 256.

ii

Credits cont.

Barbara Zimmerman, President, BZ/Rights & Permissions, Inc., in securing the rights and permissions for the fine art.

Donald Norsworthy, for photography of Mr. Art and Music Expressions™ characters.

West Music, for providing rhythm instrument photos.

Dr. Artie Almeida and Bear Lake Elementary School, for the use of Orff performance photographs.

Steve Palm, Vice President, Scholastic Marketing Partners, Scholastic Inc., for marketing consultation.

Gino Silva, Art Director, Scholastic Marketing Partners, Scholastic Inc., for cover and logo designs.

The New World Symphony, America's Orchestral Academy, Michael Tilson Thomas, artistic director, for the courtesy of providing photos on pages 96 and 240.

The Thanh Cam Musical Instrument Workshop (www.thanhcammusic.com), Hanoi, Vietnam, for the photo of the Dàn Bàu on page 251.

Gibson Musical Instruments, for the courtesy of providing a photo of F5 Master Model Mandolin on page 216.

ILLUSTRATION CREDITS
(Student Edition page/Teacher Edition page)

1/4. Robert Ramsay
2–5/6. Thais Yanes
6–9/8. Olivia Novak
12–13/10. Martha Ramirez
14–15/15. Ken Rehm
16–17/16. Candy Woolley
18–19/16. Martha Ramirez
20–21/20. Lisa Greene Mane
22–25/22. Jeannette Aquino
26–27/24. Nancy Rehm
28–29/24. Lisa Greene Mane
30–31/27. Melody Bryan
32–35/32–33. Cesar Tuc Hernandez
39/36. Thais Yanes
40–41/40. Jeannette Aquino
44–45/42. Henry Hughes
46–47/44. Jeannette Aquino
49/45. Thais Yanes
50–51/50. Ken Rehm
54–55/52. Lisa Greene Mane
56–57/54. Martha Ramirez
60–61/60. Ernesto Ebanks
62–63/61. Martha Ramirez
64–65/62. Ernesto Ebanks
66–67/64. Robert Ramsay
72–73/66. Lisa Greene Mane
74–75/68. Martha Ramirez
76–77/69. Lisa Greene Mane
78–79/74. Ken Rehm
80–81/75. Candy Woolley
82–83/76. Martha Ramirez
84–87/78–79. Rama Hughes
88–89/80. Martha Ramirez
94–95/85. Thais Yanes
96–97/86. Lisa Greene Mane/ Janel Harrison

100–101/89. Natalie Auth
102–103/94. Thais Yanes
104–105/96. Candy Woolley
106–107/98. Candy Woolley/ Melody Bryan
110–111/100. Ernesto Ebanks
112–113/101. Ken Rehm
114–115/105. Judit Martinez
116–117/107. Henry Hughes
118–119/108. Robert Ramsay
120–121/114. Nancy Rehm
122–123/115. Lisa Greene Mane
124–125/117. Judit Martinez
126–127/119. Ernesto Ebanks
132–133/121. Magdi Rodriguez
134–135/124. Robert Ramsay
138–139/126. Ken Rehm
142–143/128. Rama Hughes
144–145/132. Martha Ramirez
146–147/139. Lisa Greene Mane
148–149/140. Jeannette Aquino
150–151/140. Thais Yanes
152–153/141. Lisa Greene Mane
154–155/148. Judit Martinez
156–157/150. Lisa Greene Mane
158–159/151. Olivia Novak
160–161/152. Robert Ramsay
164–165/156. Lisa Greene Mane
166–167/158. Robert Ramsay
170–171/160. Lisa Greene Mane
172–173/164. Ken Rehm
174–175/170. Ken Rehm
176–177/177. Ernesto Ebanks
178–179/177. Candy Woolley
180–181/178. Judit Martinez
182–183/179. Thais Yanes
186–187/183. Henry Hughes
188–189/184. Ernesto Ebanks
190–191/188. Lisa Greene Mane
192–193/189. Ken Rehm
194–195/190. Rama Hughes
196–197/191. Rama Hughes
200–201/194. Martha Ramirez
202–203/195. Robert Ramsay
204–205/198. Ernesto Ebanks
206–207/199. Thais Yanes
208–209/201. Robert Ramsay
210–211/208. Ernesto Ebanks
212–213/209. Robert Ramsay
216–217/214. Judit Martinez
220–221/216. Robert Ramsay
224–225/217. Shawn Martinez
226–227/220. Rama Hughes
228–229/224. Thais Yanes
230–231/225. Rama Hughes
234–235/228. Candy Woolley
236–237/229. Judit Martinez
240–241/234. Ernesto Ebanks
244–245/241. Natalie Auth
248–249/246. Thais Yanes
250–251/248. Thais Yanes
254–255/254. Lisa Greene Mane
258–259/256. Martha Ramirez

260–261/257. Lisa Greene Mane
262–263/258. Candy Woolley
266–267/267. Lisa Greene Mane
268–269/271. Candy Woolley
272–273/272. Jeannette Aquino
274–275/274. Nancy Rehm
276–277/275. Ernesto Ebanks
278–279/276. Rama Hughes
280–281/277. Rama Hughes
284–285/282. Jeannette Aquino
288–289/284. Natalie Auth
290–291/286. Martha Ramirez
292–293/287. Rama Hughes
294–295/292. Rama Hughes
296–297/293. Henry Hughes
298–299/294. Candy Woolley
306–307/297. Natalie Auth
156–157/303. Lisa Greene Mane
308–309/314. Nancy Rehm
310–311/315. Nancy Rehm
312–313/316. Robert Ramsay

314–315/318. Janel Harrison/ Candy Woolley
316–317/322. Olivia Novak
318–319/324. Natalie Auth
320–321/325. Ernesto Ebanks
322–323/326. Martha Ramirez
324–325/327. Thais Yanes

PHOTO CREDITS
(Student Edition page/Teacher Edition page)

10/9. Woody Guthrie: © Bettmann/Corbis
42/41. Ottmar Liebert: © Reisig & Taylor
58/54. Sweet Honey in the Rock: © Dwight Carter
78–79/74. Boston Pops: © Michael Lutch; Balalaika Orchestra: © Bettmann/Corbis
94–95/85. Marine Band: United States Marine Band; Candlelit Choir: © Bob Krist/Corbis
97/86. Candlelit Choir: © Bob Krist/Corbis
98/86. Samuel Barber: © Bettmann/Corbis
128/119. Reba McEntire: Photograph by George Holz
140/126. Claude Debussy: © Bettmann/Corbis
168/160. Dave Brubeck: © Tony Stone Images, Stephen Johnson
206–207/199. Sonor Orff instruments provided courtesy of Hohner, Inc./HSS
214/209. Yo-Yo Ma: © Reuters NewMedia Inc./Corbis
216–217/214. John Hartford: © Neal Preston/Corbis; Performance of "O Brother Where Art Thou": © Reuters NewMedia Inc./Corbis; Master Model Mandolin Courtesy Gibson Musical Instruments
222/216. Cynthia Phelps: Photo: J. Henry Fair
234–235/228. String Quartet: © Steve Raymer/Corbis
238/230. Antonio Vivaldi: © Bettmann/Corbis
242/236. Yehudi Menuhin: © AFP/Corbis; Ray Brown: © AFP/Corbis; Stephane Grappelli: © John Van Hasselt/Corbis Sygma; George Benson: © Derick A. Thomas; Dat's Jazz/Corbis
248/246. © Kelly-Mooney Photography/Corbis
250–251/248. Sitar: © AFP/Corbis; Koto: © Corbis; Welsh Harp: © Ted Spiegel/Corbis; Koto: © Bob Krist/Corbis; Dàn Bàu: Thanh Cam Musical Instrument Workshop, Hanoi, Vietnam (www.thanhcammusic.com)
254/254. Koto: © Kelly-Mooney Photography/Corbis
256/255. Photo courtesy of Minoru Miki
260–261/257. Kabuki Theater: © Reuters NewMedia Inc./Corbis; Kabuki Performance: © Michael S. Yamashita/Corbis; Traditional Japanese Tea Ceremony: © Royalty-Free/Corbis; Koto: © Corbis
282/279. Morton Gould: © Bettmann/Corbis
298–299/294. © Ken Reid/Getty Images
300/295. Benjamin Britten: © Hulton-Deutsch Collection/Corbis
302/296. Johann Sebastian Bach: © Bettmann/Corbis

Warner Bros. Publications has made every effort to locate and appropriately credit copyright owners of all materials in this series. We would appreciate any errors or omissions be brought to our attention, and corrections will be made.

Fine Art Credits

Whirligig, entitled "America," c. 1938–42. Frank Memkus, American, 1895–1965. Wood and metal (height with paddle up): 80 3/4 x 29 x 40 in. Restricted gift of Marshall Field, Mr. and Mrs. Robert A. Kubiceck, Mr. James Raoul Simmons, Mrs. Esther Sparks, Mrs. Frank L. Sulzberger, and the Oak Park–River Forest Associates of the Woman's Board of The Art Institute of Chicago, 1980.166. Photo © The Art Institute of Chicago.
> pg. 36 Student Edition   pg. 34 Teacher Edition

Flags on 57th Street, Winter 1918 by Frederick Childe Hassam (1859–1935). Oil on linen. 94 x 6 3/5 cm. New York Historical Society, New York, USA/Bridgeman Art Library.
> pg. 37 Student Edition   pg. 34 Teacher Edition

Miss Liberty by Edward Ambrose. Collection of Meadow Farm Museum, County of Henrico, Virginia. All Rights Reserved.
> pg. 38 Student Edition   pg. 35 Teacher Edition

Life's Phases by Sue Hovey. Mixed media on canvas 48 x 36 in. © Sue Hovey.
> pg. 48 Student Edition   pg. 45 Teacher Edition

Dance on the Beach (1900–02) by Edvard Munch (1863–1944). © 2003 The Munch Museum/The Munch–Ellingsen Group/Artist Rights Society (ARS), NY. Transparency: © Erich Lessing/Art Resource, NY.
> pg. 52 Student Edition   pg. 52 Teacher Edition

Portrait of Mrs. Cherkasov with her son Alexander. Zinaida Serebriakova (1884–1967). Russian State Museum, St. Petersburg, Russia. Transparency: © Scala/Art Resource, NY.
> pg. 70 Student Edition   pg. 65 Teacher Edition

Cats in Paris. Sandy Skoglund. Photolithograph. 20 x 25.5 in. © 1993 Sandy Skoglund.
> pg. 90 Student Edition   pg. 80 Teacher Edition

Flag Raising in New York City after 9/11/01. © 2001 *The Record* (Bergen County, NJ), Thomas E. Franklin, Staff Photographer.
> pg. 92 Student Edition   pg. 84 Teacher Edition

The Sleeping Beauty—Houston Ballet by Drew Donovan. Photograph. Dancer: Lauren Anderson. © 2002 Drew Donovan.
> pg. 108 Student Edition   pg. 99 Teacher Edition

The Banjo Lesson (1893) by Henry O. Tanner (1859–1937). Oil on canvas. 49 x 35 1/2 in. Hampton University Museum, Hampton, Virginia.
> pg. 130 Student Edition   pg. 120 Teacher Edition

Cakewalk by Carmen Lomas Garza. Acrylic painting. 36 x 48 in. © 1987 Carmen Lomas Garza. Photo credit: M. Lee Fatherree.
> pg. 136 Student Edition   pg. 125 Teacher Edition

Turkey Feathers and Indian Pot (1941) by Georgia O'Keeffe (1887–1986). Oil on canvas, 20 x 16 in. Photo Courtesy of Spanierman Gallery, New York.
> pg. 198 Student Edition   pg. 192 Teacher Edition

Violin, by Stradivari, Cremona, 1699 by Stradivari (1644–1737). Victoria & Albert Museum, London, UK/Bridgeman Art Library.
> pg. 218 Student Edition   pg. 215 Teacher Edition

Celestial Quartet by Jim Stallings. © Jim Stallings.
> pg. 219 Student Edition   pg. 215 Teacher Edition

Gregory & Maurice Hines. Photograph. © Bettmann/Corbis.
> pg. 232 Student Edition   pg. 227 Teacher Edition

Three Flags, 1958. Jasper Johns (b. 1930). Encaustic on canvas. 30 7/8 x 45 1/2 x 5 in (78.42 x 115.57 x 12.7 cm). © Jasper Johns/Licensed by VAGA, New York, NY. Transparency: Collection of Whitney Museum of American Art, New York; 50th Anniversary Gift of the Gilman Foundation, Inc., The Lauder Foundation, A. Alfred Taubman, an anonymous donor, and purchase.
> pg. 246 Student Edition   pg. 241 Teacher Edition

Lute and Molecule No. 2, 1958. Ben Shahn (1898–1969). Serigraph with watercolor. 25 1/4 x 38 3/4 in. © Estate of Ben Shahn/Licensed by VAGA, New York, NY. Transparency: New Jersey State Museum Collection, purchase, FA1969.288.11.
> pg. 252 Student Edition   pg. 249 Teacher Edition

Mochibana (Rice Cake and Flowers) by Keiko Kodai. 17 x 12 1/2 in. © 2002 The Wing Gallery.
> pg. 264 Student Edition   pg. 264 Teacher Edition

Sky and Water I (1938) by M. C. Escher (1898–1972). 55 x 65 cm. © 2002 Cordon Art B. V. –Baarn –Holland. All rights reserved.
> pg. 270 Student Edition   pg. 271 Teacher Edition

Eggs Encircled, 1948. Carlotta M. Corpron. Gelatin silver print, 9 9/16 x 7 13/16 in. © 1988, Amon Carter Museum, Fort Worth. Gift of the artist.
> pg. 286 Student Edition   pg. 283 Teacher Edition

Brushstroke (1965) by Roy Lichtenstein (1923–1997). Screenprint on heavy white wove paper, sheet 23 x 29 in. (58.4 x 73.6 cm); image 22 3/16 x 28 1/2 in. (56.4 x 72.3 cm). © Estate of Roy Lichtenstein.
> pg. 304 Student Edition   pg. 296 Teacher Edition

Contents

Maestro

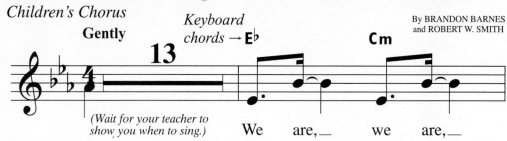

Children of the World

Children's Chorus

Gently

Keyboard chords → **E♭**

By BRANDON BARNES
and ROBERT W. SMITH

(Wait for your teacher to show you when to sing.)

We are,___ we are,___

we are___ the chil - dren.___ We are,___ we are,___

we are___ the chil - dren.___

(Wait for your teacher to show you when to sing.)

We are___ the chil - dren,___ chil-dren of___ the world.

We are___ the chil - dren,___ chil-dren of___ the world.

We are,___ we are,___ we are___ the chil - dren.___

4   © 2003 BEAM ME UP MUSIC (ASCAP)   All Rights Administered by WARNER BROS. PUBLICATIONS U.S. INC.   All Rights Reserved

We are,— we are,— we are— the chil - dren.—

Driving!

4

(Wait for your teacher to show you when to sing.)

We are,— we are,—

we are— the chil - dren.— We are,— we are,—

we are— the chil - dren.— We are— the chil - dren,—

Soaring!

chil - dren of— the world. We are— the chil - dren,—

chil - dren of— the world. We are— the chil - dren,—

chil - dren of the world!—

5

This Land Is Your Land

Words and Music by
WOODY GUTHRIE
Arranged by MICHAEL STORY

Refrain:

This land is your land,____ this land is my land,____ from Cal - i - for - nia____ to the New York Is - land;____ from the red - wood for - est____ to the Gulf Stream wa - ters;____

To Verse
End here last time

this land was made for you and me.

TRO – © 1956, 1958, 1970 and 1972 LUDLOW MUSIC, INC., New York, NY   Copyrights Renewed   All Rights Reserved   Used by Permission

Verse:

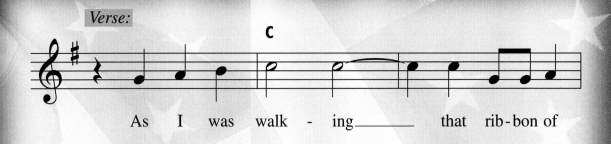

As I was walk - ing   that rib-bon of

high - way,   I saw a - bove me

_ that end - less sky - way,   I saw be -

low me   that gold - en val - ley,

To Refrain

this land was made for you and me.

9

Woody Guthrie

Woody Guthrie

(1912–1967)

Woody (Woodrow Wilson) Guthrie was born July 14, 1912, in Okemah, Oklahoma. His father was a cowboy. Woody often felt as if he did not belong. Some of his songs were very sad. He played guitar and wrote songs such as "This Land Is Your Land." Woody's songs, ballads, and poetry are still performed.

Skip, Step, Repeated Tone Game

skips

The distance from one tone to a tone that is more than a step away from it

steps

The distance from one tone to the tone next to it

repeated tones

Tones that are the same and occur more than once

Skip up

Skip down

Step up

Step down

Repeat

Repeat

This Land Is Your Land

Words and Music by
WOODY GUTHRIE
Arranged by MICHAEL STORY

Refrain:

This land is your land,____ this land is

my land,____ from Cal - i - for - nia____

__ to the New York Is - land;____

__ from the red - wood for - est____

__ to the Gulf Stream wa - ters;____

To Verse
End here last time

this land was made for you and me.

TRO – © 1956, 1958, 1970 and 1972 LUDLOW MUSIC, INC., New York, NY   Copyrights Renewed   All Rights Reserved   Used by Permission

Play the Steady Beat

The steady beat does not get faster or slower

quart   quart   2-eight   quart

repeated pattern

A pattern that occurs more than once

ostinato
A repeated melodic or rhythmic pattern that occurs several times

Yo!

stomp

jun

dance

MALI

BU

GUINEA

IVORY COAST

G

LIBERIA

Atlantic Oce

N

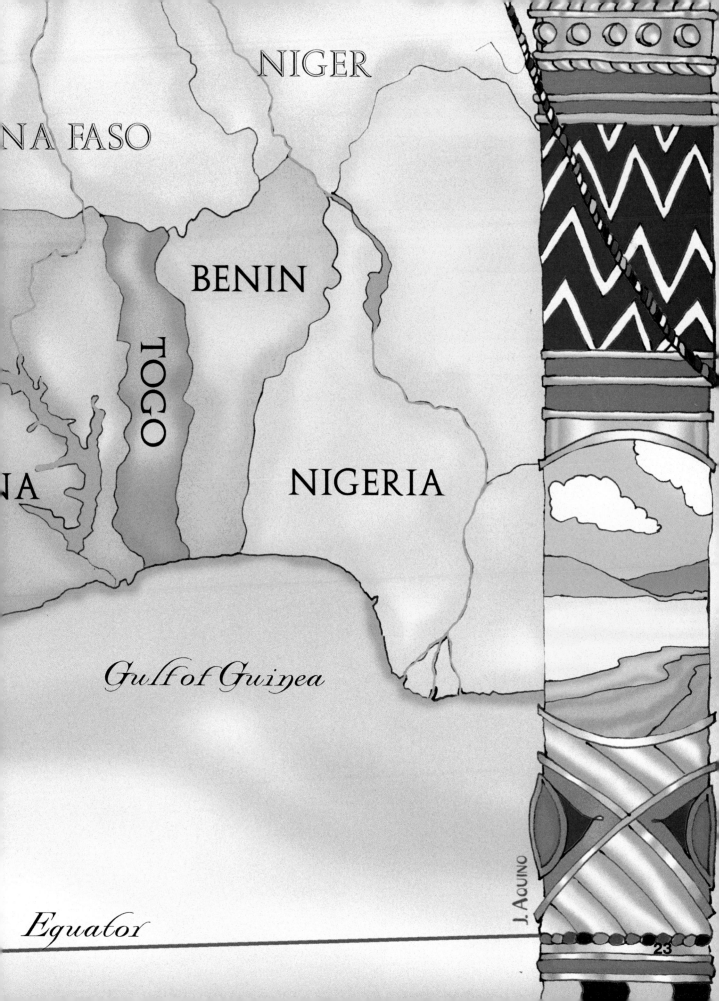

Tap — Tap — Pa-ss

25 J. Aquino

Learn a Square Dance

Square

Swing

Promenade

THIS LAND IS YOUR LAND

Words and Music by
WOODY GUTHRIE
Arranged by MICHAEL STORY

Refrain:

This land is your land,____ this land is my land,____ from Cal - i - for - nia ____ to the New York Is - land;____ from the red - wood for - est ____ to the Gulf Stream wa - ters;____

To Verse
End here last time

this land was made for you and me.

TRO – © 1956, 1958, 1970 and 1972 LUDLOW MUSIC, INC., New York, NY   Copyrights Renewed   All Rights Reserved   Used by Permission

Refrain:
This land is your land, this land is my land,
From California to the New York Island;
From the redwood forest to the Gulf Stream waters;
This land was made for you and me.

Verse 1:
As I was walking that ribbon of highway,
I saw above me that endless skyway,
I saw below me that golden valley,
This land was made for you and me.

Refrain

Verse 2:
I've roamed and rambled and I've followed my footsteps
To the sparkling sands of her diamond deserts,
And all around me a voice was sounding,
This land was made for you and me.

Refrain

Verse 3:
The sun comes shining as I was strolling
The wheat fields waving and the dust clouds rolling.
The fog was lifting, a voice come chanting,
This land was made for you and me.

Expressive

expressive singing
Shows the mood or feeling of the song

America

patriotic music

Music that helps us express
our love for our country

American Patriotic Sing-Along

("America"; "America, the Beautiful"; and "You're a Grand Old Flag")

Adapted and Arranged by
MICHAEL STORY

"America"

My coun - try, 'tis of thee, sweet land of lib - er - ty, of thee I sing. Land where my fa - thers died, land of the pil - grims' pride, from ev - 'ry___ moun - tain-side, let___ free - dom ring!

"America, the Beautiful"

O beau - ti - ful for spa - cious skies, for

© 2003 BEAM ME UP MUSIC (ASCAP)   All Rights Administered by WARNER BROS. PUBLICATIONS U.S. INC.   All Rights Reserved

am - ber waves of grain, for pur - ple moun - tain

maj - es - ties, a - bove the fruit - ed plain. A -

mer - i - ca! A - mer - i - ca! God shed His grace on

thee, and crown thy good with broth - er - hood, from

sea to shin - ing sea.

"You're a Grand Old Flag"*

You're a grand old flag, you're a

high - fly - ing flag, and for - ev - er in

*By George M. Cohan

peace may you wave._____ You're the em - blem

of the land I love, the home of the

free and the brave._____ Ev - 'ry heart beats

true 'neath the red, white, and blue, where there's

nev - er a boast or brag;_____ but should

auld ac - quain - tance be for - got, keep your

eye on the grand old flag._____

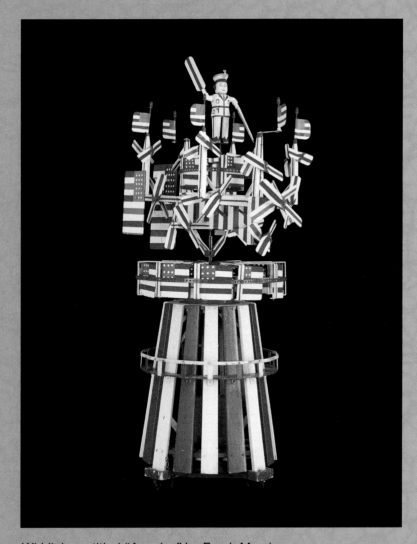

Whirligig, entitled "America" by Frank Memkus

- **This is a whirligig. How would you describe a whirligig?**

- **What familiar patriotic symbol did the artist use to create the whirligig?**

- **How are the flags used here different from our American flag at school?**

Flags on 57th Street, Winter 1918 by Frederick Childe Hassam

- **Is this a painting or a sculpture?**

- **How can you tell?**

- **What do you think is happening in this picture?**

- **On what special occasions do we fly flags?**

Miss Liberty by Edward Ambrose

- **Is this a painting or a sculpture?**

- **How do you know?**

- **Why do you think the artist named this sculpture *Miss Liberty*?**

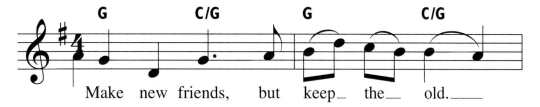

Make New Friends

TRADITIONAL FRIENDSHIP SONG
Arranged by MICHAEL STORY

| G | C/G | G | C/G |

Make new friends, but keep_ the_ old._

| G | C/G | G/D | D7 | G |

One is sil-ver, and the oth – er gold.

© 2003 BEAM ME UP MUSIC (ASCAP)   All Rights Administered by WARNER BROS. PUBLICATIONS U.S. INC.   All Rights Reserved

diction

Pronouncing words correctly and clearly when speaking or singing

Barcelona Nights

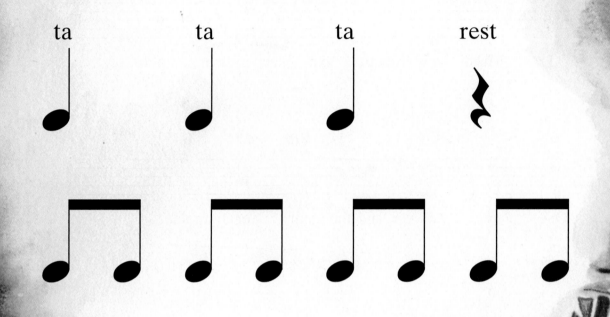

ta   ta   ta   rest

Ottmar Liebert

Photo: Reisig & Taylor

Ottmar Liebert

(b. 1963)

Ottmar Liebert was born in Cologne, Germany. He began playing guitar at the age of 11 and completed a course in classical guitar when he was 18. Later, Ottmar moved to Boston, where he performed in several jazz and rock bands. From Boston, he moved to Santa Fe, New Mexico. The music he writes combines Spanish guitar style with Brazilian dance rhythms and modern electric instruments. The name of his band is Luna Negra. His album, *Nouveau Flamenco*, pronounced *noo-voh flah-mehn-koh*, is the biggest selling guitar album of all time.

Hello

HELLO

Hello

HELLO

HELLO

Hello

Hello

Hello

Hello

Hello

HELLO

Hello

body percussion

Sounds that are produced by actions such as clapping, snapping, and stomping

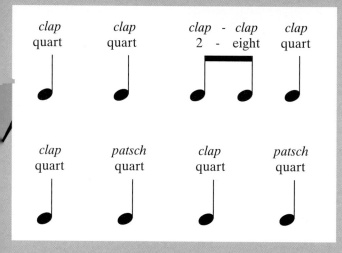

| *clap*
quart | *clap*
quart | *clap - clap*
2 - eight | *clap*
quart |
| *clap*
quart | *patsch*
quart | *clap*
quart | *patsch*
quart |

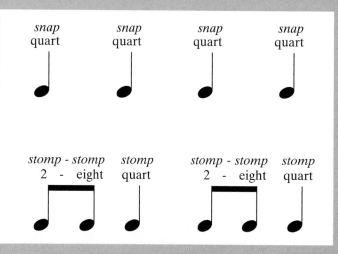

| *snap*
quart | *snap*
quart | *snap*
quart | *snap*
quart |
| *stomp - stomp*
2 - eight | *stomp*
quart | *stomp - stomp*
2 - eight | *stomp*
quart |

Life's Phases by Sue Hovey

- **Which of the horses best matches the style of the song "All the Pretty Little Horses"?**

- **Why?**

- **How are the horses different from each other?**

- **How are they alike?**

All the Pretty Little Horses

HAUNTING LULLABY
SOUTHERN UNITED STATES
Arranged by ROBERT W. SMITH

Phrase 1

Cm   Fm

Hush - a - by, don't you cry.

B♭   Cm

Go to sleep - y, lit - tle ba — by.

Phrase 2

Fm

When you wake, you shall have

B♭   Cm

all the pret - ty lit - tle hors — es.

Phrase 3

Gm   Cm

Blacks and bays, dap - ples and grays,

B♭   Cm

coach and six - a lit - tle hors — es.

Phrase 4

Fm

Hush - a - by, don't you cry.

B♭   Cm

Go to sleep - y, lit - tle ba — by.

© 2003 BEAM ME UP MUSIC (ASCAP)   All Rights Administered by WARNER BROS. PUBLICATIONS U.S. INC.   All Rights Reserved

Make New Friends

G   C/G   G   C/G

Make new friends, but keep_ the_ old.__

mi
re
do

G   C/G   G/D D 7 G

One is sil - ver, and the oth - er gold.

© 2003 BEAM ME UP MUSIC (ASCAP) All Rights Administered by WARNER BROS. PUBLICATIONS U.S. INC. All Rights Reserved

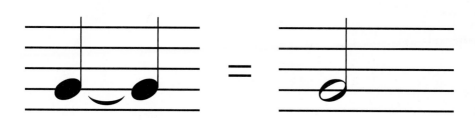

half note

**Two quarter notes tied together.
A half note is twice the length
of a quarter note.**

Dance on the Beach by Edvard Munch

- What do you see in this artwork?

- What shape does the tree in the picture create?

- Is this shape like phrases in music?

- If you could name it, what would you call this artwork? Why?

This Land Is Your Land

Words and Music by
WOODY GUTHRIE

Refrain:

This land is your land, this land is

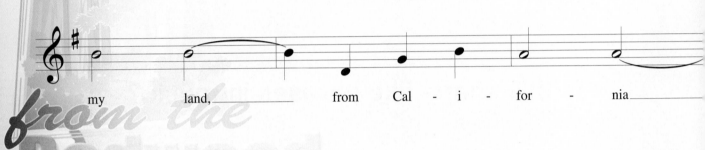

my land, from Cal - i - for - nia

to the New York Is - land; from the red - wood

for - est to the Gulf Stream wa - ters;

this land was made for you and me.

TRO – © 1956, 1958, 1970 and 1972 LUDLOW MUSIC, INC., New York, NY
Copyrights Renewed
All Rights Reserved   Used by Permission

this land is my land

Verse:

As I was walk - ing_____ that rib - bon of

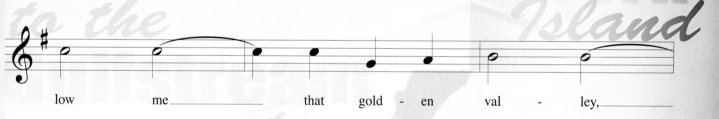

high - way,_____ I saw a - bove me_____

____ that end - less sky - way,_____ I saw be -

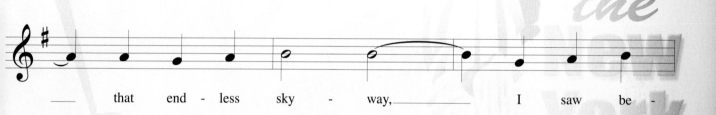

low me_____ that gold - en val - ley,_____

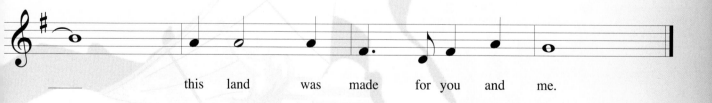

____ this land was made for you and me.

melodic rhythm
The rhythm of the words

steady beat
The repeated even pulse of music

Left to right: Aisha Kahlil, Nitanju Bolade Casel, Bernice Johnson Reagon, Carol Maillard, Shirley Childress Saxton, and Ysaye Maria Barnwell

Photo: Dwight Carter

Sweet Honey in the Rock

Sweet Honey in the Rock is a Grammy® Award–winning ensemble of African-American women. Their first album was released in 1976. The name *Sweet Honey in the Rock* comes from a Bible story that tells of a land so rich that when rocks were cracked open, honey flowed from them. The women in this group consider themselves to be as strong as a rock and as sweet as honey. Their music comes from deep roots in the sacred music of the black church—spirituals, hymns, and gospel—as well as jazz and blues. The artists compose, arrange, and perform songs with strong messages about the world they live in and the issues that concern them.

bar line
A line that goes from the bottom to the top of a staff and divides the staff into measures

measure
A group of beats separated by bar lines

meter
The repeated pattern of beats per measure

America

TRADITIONAL ENGLISH MELODY
Words by SAMUEL FRANCIS SMITH
Arranged by MICHAEL STORY

My coun - try 'tis of thee,

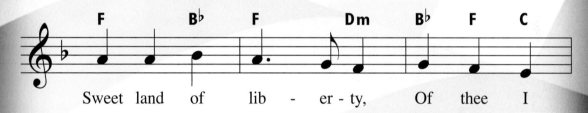

Sweet land of lib - er - ty, Of thee I

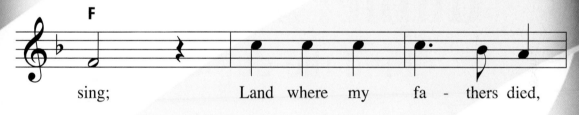

sing; Land where my fa - thers died,

Land of the Pil - grims' pride, From ev - 'ry__

moun - tain side, Let__ free - dom ring!

© 2003 BEAM ME UP MUSIC (ASCAP)   All Rights Administered by WARNER BROS. PUBLICATIONS U.S. INC.   All Rights Reserved

duple: Set of two

Find the duples.

triple: Set of three
Find the triples.

Old Woman

TRADITIONAL
Arranged by JACK BULLOCK

Verse: Boys **D**

sol   *mi*   *do*

f 1. Old wom - an, old wom - an,
2. Old wom - an, old wom - an,
3. Old wom - an, old wom - an,
p 4. Old wom - an, old wom - an,

A7   **D**

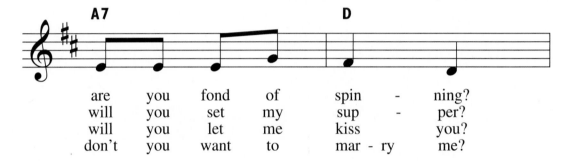

are you fond of spin - ning?
will you set my sup - per?
will you let me kiss you?
don't you want to mar - ry me?

Old wom - an, old wom - an,
Old wom - an, old wom - an,
Old wom - an, old wom - an,
Old wom - an, old wom - an,

A7   **D**

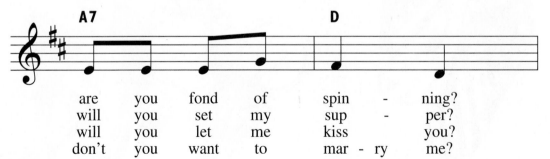

are you fond of spin - ning?
will you set my sup - per?
will you let me kiss you?
don't you want to mar - ry me?

© 2003 BEAM ME UP MUSIC (ASCAP) All Rights Administered by WARNER BROS. PUBLICATIONS U.S. INC. All Rights Reserved

Refrain: Girls

mf Speak a lit - tle loud - er, sir, I'm
Speak a lit - tle loud - er, sir, I'm
Speak a lit - tle loud - er, sir, I
f Oh, my good - ness, gra - cious me, I

A7   D

ver - y hard of hear - ing.
ver - y hard of hear - ing.
just be - gin to hear you.
hear you now quite clear - ly.

Speak a lit - tle loud - er, sir, I'm
Speak a lit - tle loud - er, sir, I'm
Speak a lit - tle loud - er, sir, I
Oh, my good - ness, gra - cious me, I

A7   D

ver - y hard of hear - ing.
ver - y hard of hear - ing.
just be - gin to hear you.
hear you now quite clear - ly.

Star Light, Star Bright

By TOSSI AARON
Arranged by ROBERT W. SMITH

Canon

Star — light, — star —
bright, first star I see — to - night, I
wish I may, — I wish I might, —
have — the wish I wish to - night.

© 1982 TOSSI AARON   All Rights Reserved   Used by Permission

Tossi Aaron

Tossi Aaron

Tossi Aaron was born in the United States. She is
an Orff Schulwerk*–trained music teacher who
writes about and teaches American folk music and
folklore. Her "Star Light, Star Bright" was written
for a music workshop in Indiana. Her background
in folk music and performing includes three
albums of folk music and appearances on several
American folk festival albums. She has written
four books for Orff music teaching. She is also a
regular presenter at the American Orff-Schulwerk
Association's national conferences. Tossi received
the Distinguished Service Award from AOSA
for 2003.

*Ask your teacher about Orff Schulwerk.

Portrait of Mrs. Cherkasov with her son Alexander by Zinaida Serebriakova

- **What do you see in this picture?**

- **How does this artwork relate to the song "Star Light, Star Bright"?**

- **If you were the artist, what would you call this picture?**

Oh, How Lovely Is the Evening

Oh, How Lovely Is the Evening

TRADITIONAL GERMAN MELODY
Arranged by JACK BULLOCK

© 2003 BEAM ME UP MUSIC (ASCAP)   All Rights Administered by WARNER BROS. PUBLICATIONS U.S. INC.   All Rights Reserved

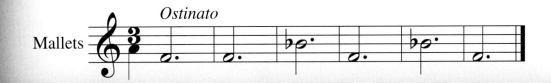

 pitty
pitty
me

 quack
quack

woof

moo

baaah

 momma
momma

74

Bought Me a Cat

SOUTHERN UNITED STATES
Arranged by MICHAEL STORY

1. I bought me a cat, the cat pleased me, I

fed my cat un-der yon-der tree, the cat went

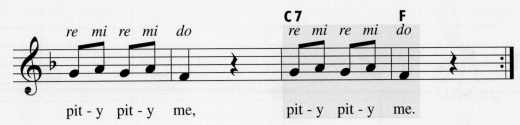

re mi re mi do pit - y pit - y me, re mi re mi do pit - y pit - y me.

© 2003 BEAM ME UP MUSIC (ASCAP)   All Rights Administered by WARNER BROS. PUBLICATIONS U.S. INC.   All Rights Reserved

re mi re mi do

Q. Question and

Here is the question.

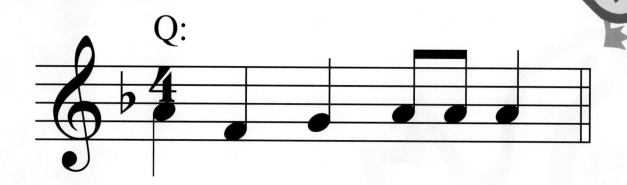

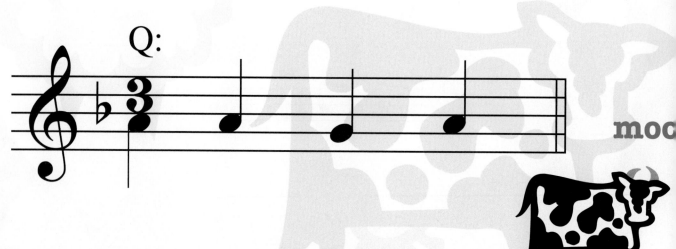

A.

What is your answer?

quack
quack

woof

do re do

pity
pity
me pity
pity
me

mi re do

mi re do-do do

momma
momma

The Star Spangled Banner

improvise
Create music
on the spot
within guidelines

80

Oh, How Lovely Is the Evening

Sarasponda

DUTCH SPINNING SONG
Arranged by MICHAEL STORY

© 2003 BEAM ME UP MUSIC (ASCAP)   All Rights Administered by WARNER BROS. PUBLICATIONS U.S. INC.   All Rights Reserved

AB form

A musical form with
two different sections

83

When I First Came to This Land

Words and Music by
OSCAR BRAND
Arranged by ROBERT W. SMITH

Verse:

D   **G**   **D**

do   mi   sol   sol

1. When   I   first   came   to   this   land,

2.-5. *See words for Verses 2-5 below.*

A   **D**   **A**   **D**

I   was   not   a   wealth-y   man.   So   I bought my-

G   **D**   **A**   **D**

self   a   farm.   I   did   what   I   could.

TRO – © 1957 and 1965 LUDLOW MUSIC, INC., New York, NY   Copyrights Renewed   All Rights Reserved   Used by Permission

2. When I first came to this land,
   I was not a wealthy man.
   So I bought myself a shack. I did what I could.
   And I called my shack "Break My Back."
   And I called my farm "Muscle In My Arm."
   But the land was sweet and good,
   And I did what I could.

3. When I first came to this land,
   I was not a wealthy man.
   So I bought myself a cow. I did what I could.
   And I called my cow "No Milk Now."
   And I called my shack "Break My Back."
   And I called my farm "Muscle In My Arm."
   But the land was sweet and good,
   And I did what I could.

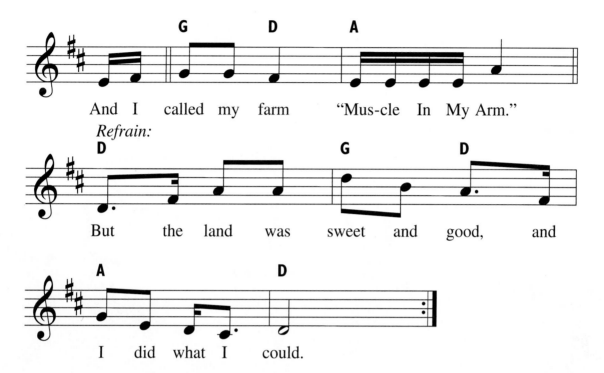

And I called my farm "Mus-cle In My Arm."

Refrain:

But the land was sweet and good, and

I did what I could.

4. When I first came to this land,
   I was not a wealthy man.
   So I bought myself a duck. I did what I could.
   And I called my duck "Out Of Luck."
   And I called my cow "No Milk Now."
   And I called my shack "Break My Back."
   And I called my farm "Muscle In My Arm."
   But the land was sweet and good,
   And I did what I could.

5. When I first came to this land,
   I was not a wealthy man.
   So I got myself a wife. I did what I could.
   And I called my wife "Love Of My Life."
   And I called my duck "Out Of Luck."
   And I called my cow "No Milk Now."
   And I called my shack "Break My Back."
   And I called my farm "Muscle In My Arm."
   But the land was sweet and good,
   And I did what I could.

Ventiquattro Gattí Blu

(Twenty-four Blue Cats)

SONG FROM ITALY

English Translation:
Twenty-four blue cats
With their tails up and their whiskers down,
All in line, three by three,
Are marching with me.

Cats in Paris by Sandy Skoglund

- How does this artwork relate to "Ventiquattro Gattí Blu"?

- How many cats do you see?

- Are the cats real?

- How do you think the artist created this scene?

Flag Raising in New York City after 9/11/01
The Record (Bergen County, NJ)

- **Have you ever seen this photograph?**

- **Where do you think this photograph was taken?**

- **Why do you think the men placed the flag at the site of the World Trade Center disaster?**

"The President's Own"
United States Marine Band

94

The Star Spangled Banner

Words by FRANCIS SCOTT KEY
Arranged by ROBERT W. SMITH

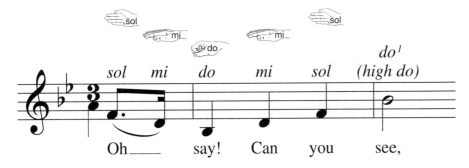

sol   mi   do   mi   sol   do¹
(high do)

Oh___ say! Can you see,

© 2003 BEAM ME UP MUSIC (ASCAP)   All Rights Administered by WARNER BROS. PUBLICATIONS U.S. INC.   All Rights Reserved

"The President's Own"
United States Marine Band

band

A large group of musicians who play wind and percussion instruments together, with no string instruments

Samuel Barber

George Frideric Handel

Samuel Barber

(1910–1981)

Samuel Barber was born in the United States. He began to compose at the age of seven. He wrote music for opera, ballet, orchestra, band, choral, vocal, and keyboard. His *Adagio for Strings* is one of his most famous pieces and can be heard in several movies. His 1957 opera *Vanessa* won the Pulitzer Prize, a very special award given to a composer for a work that has been selected as the most outstanding of its type for the year.

George Frideric Handel

(1685–1759)

George Frideric Handel was born in Hamburg, Germany, and also lived in Italy and England. His father was a barber-surgeon who wanted him to become a lawyer. At first he practiced secretly, but his father finally allowed him to study music. Handel wrote many vocal works in Italian. He is especially famous for his choral work *Messiah*. The "Hallelujah Chorus" is often performed at Christmas and Easter. It is part of *Messiah*. Handel spent the last several years of his life blind. He died in 1759 and was buried in Westminster Abbey.

Coffee Grows o

EARLY AMERICAN PLAY-PARTY SONG
Arranged by ROBERT W. SMITH

A Gentle waltz

do mi sol la sol mi do

Cof - fee grows on white oak trees, the

riv - er flows with hon - ey - o. Go

choose some - one to roam with you, as

sweet as m'las - ses can - dy - o.

B Hoedown

Two in the mid-dle and they can't go o - ver,

two in the mid-dle and they can't go o - ver,

two in the mid-dle and they can't go o - ver,

hel - lo, Su - san Brown.

© 2003 BEAM ME UP MUSIC (ASCAP)   All Rights Administered by WARNER BROS. PUBLICATIONS U.S. INC.   All Rights Reserved

White Oak Trees

Swing you an-oth-er one and you'll get o - ver,

swing you an-oth-er one and you'll get o - ver,

swing you an-oth-er one and you'll get o - ver,

hel - lo, Su - san Brown.

Four in the mid - dle and they all go o - ver,

four in the mid - dle and they all go o - ver,

four in the mid - dle and they all go o - ver,

Yee-haw!

hel - lo, Su - san Brown.

choir/chorus
A group of singers

audience etiquette
The rules for proper behavior during a live performance

THE STAR SPANGLED BANNER

Words by FRANCIS SCOTT KEY
Arranged by ROBERT W. SMITH

© 2003 BEAM ME UP MUSIC (ASCAP)   All Rights Administered by WARNER BROS. PUBLICATIONS U.S. INC.   All Rights Reserved

(the song continues in the next lesson)

103

HEE-HAW! HEE-HAW!

SWEETLY SINGS THE DONKEY

TRADITIONAL AMERICAN ROUND
Arranged by MICHAEL STORY

1. *Man:* Sweet - ly sings the don - key
2. *Woman:* Sweet - ly sings the don - key
3. *Child:* Sweet - ly sings the don - key

at the break of day. If you don't sing
at the break of day. If you don't sing
at the break of day. If you don't sing

loud - er, you will get no hay._____ Hee -
loud - er, you will get no hay._____ Hee -
loud - er, you will get no hay._____ Hee -

haw! Hee - haw! Hee -
haw! Hee - haw! Hee -
haw! Hee - haw! Hee -

sol

haw, hee-haw, hee - haw!
haw, hee-haw, hee - haw!
haw, hee-haw, hee - haw!

do   sol do   sol   do

© 2003 BEAM ME UP MUSIC (ASCAP)   All Rights Administered by WARNER BROS. PUBLICATIONS U.S. INC.   All Rights Reserved

sol   mi   do   *sol   do*

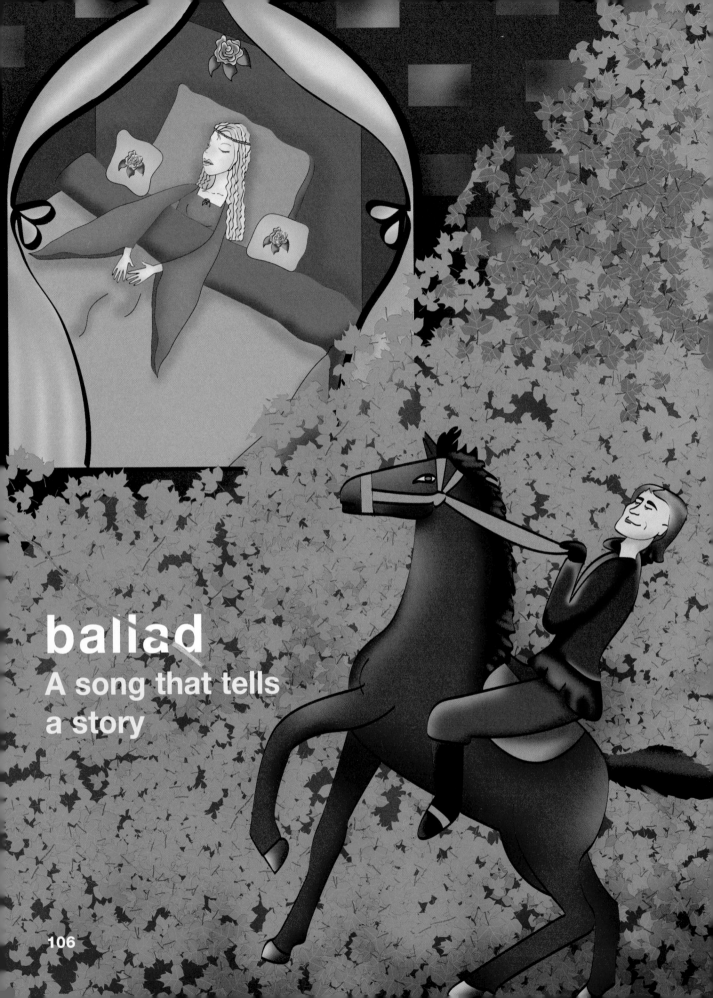

ballad
A song that tells
a story

106

Fair Rosa

IRISH BALLAD

1. Fair Ro - sa was a love - ly child, a

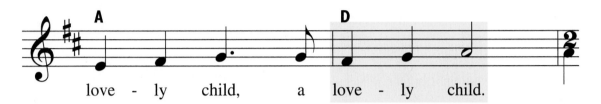

love - ly child, a love - ly child.

Fair Ro - sa was a love - ly child a

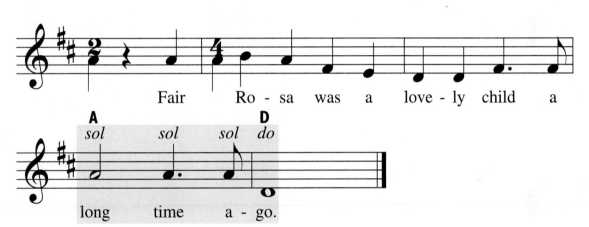

sol   sol   sol   do

long   time   a - go.

2. A wicked fairy cast a spell,
Cast a spell, cast a spell.
A wicked fairy cast a spell,
A long time ago.

3. Fair Rosa slept a hundred years,
A hundred years, a hundred years.
Fair Rosa slept a hundred years,
A long time ago.

4. The hedges, they all grew around,
Grew around, grew around.
The hedges, they all grew around,
A long time ago.

5. A handsome prince came riding by,
Riding by, riding by.
A handsome prince came riding by,
A long time ago.

6. He kissed Fair Rosa's lily-white hand,
Lily-white hand, lily-white hand.
He kissed Fair Rosa's lily-white hand,
A long time ago.

7. Fair Rosa will not sleep no more,
Sleep no more, sleep no more.
Fair Rosa will not sleep no more,
A long time ago.

© 2003 BEAM ME UP MUSIC (ASCAP)   All Rights Administered by WARNER BROS. PUBLICATIONS U.S. INC.   All Rights Reserved

107

The Sleeping Beauty—Houston Ballet
Photographer: Drew Donovan
Dancer: Lauren Anderson

- **How does this artwork relate to "Fair Rosa"?**

- **How would you describe the ballerina?**

- **What is a ballet?**

- **Have you ever been to a ballet?**

- **What would you see and hear at a ballet?**

Great Big Stars

Slowly

AFRICAN-AMERICAN SPIRITUAL
Arranged by MICHAEL STORY

1. Great big stars way up yon - der,
2. Great big moon way up yon - der,

great big stars way up yon - der,
great big moon way up yon - der,

great big stars way up yon - der,
great big moon way up yon - der,

oh, my lit - tle soul's gon - na shine, shine.

Oh, my lit - tle soul's gon - na shine, shine.

Oh, my lit - tle soul's gon - na shine, shine.

Oh, my lit - tle soul's gon - na shine, shine.

© 2003 BEAM ME UP MUSIC (ASCAP)   All Rights Administered by WARNER BROS. PUBLICATIONS U.S. INC.   All Rights Reserved

BULLDOG CHANT

American Folk Chant

Way down south in the han - ky pank, I say

bull - dog, bull - dog, han - ky pank, I say

fee, fi, fo, fum,

lis - ten to that bull - dog.

The Star Spangled Banner

Words by FRANCIS SCOTT KEY
Arranged by ROBERT W. SMITH

© 2003 BEAM ME UP MUSIC (ASCAP)   All Rights Administered by WARNER BROS. PUBLICATIONS U.S. INC.   All Rights Reserved

MARYANN ELIZABETH

TRADITIONAL MELODY
Lyrics by JUNE M. HINCKLEY
Arranged by JACK BULLOCK

Ma - ry-Ann E - liz - 'beth   Su - sie Ann Re - bec - ca

Bo — na - parte   Hot - ten - tot   Bly.

Repeat this

do¹ do¹ do¹ do¹ sol   sol sol   do¹ do¹ do¹ do¹ sol

It's a sil - ly name, but my moth-er's is the same, so I

last phrase as an ending.

guess that I will have it 'til I die.

© 2003 BEAM ME UP MUSIC (ASCAP)   All Rights Administered by WARNER BROS. PUBLICATIONS U.S. INC.   All Rights Reserved

117

Hill 'n Gully

CALYPSO FOLK SONG
Arranged by ROBERT W. SMITH

© 2003 BEAM ME UP MUSIC (ASCAP)   All Rights Administered by WARNER BROS. PUBLICATIONS U.S. INC.   All Rights Reserved

face had an ug-ly frown, hill 'n gul-ly. 'Cause he

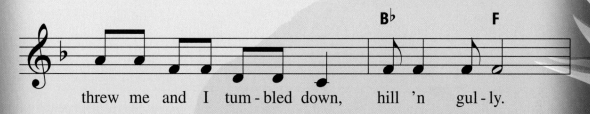

threw me and I tum-bled down, hill 'n gul-ly.

A

Hill 'n gul-ly rid-er, hill 'n gul-ly.

Last time shout: Hill 'n gully!

Hill 'n gul-ly rid-er, hill 'n gul-ly.

Star light,
Star bright...

Ah.

Star Light, Star Bright

By TOSSI AARON
Arranged by ROBERT W. SMITH

Gently

Star light, star bright, first star I see to - night, I wish I may, I wish I might, have the wish I wish to - night. wish to - night. wish to - night.

© 1982 TOSSI AARON   All Rights Reserved   Used by Permission

chord

Three or more tones sounded at the same time

whole note

pattern

123

pizzicato

Plucking the strings

arco
Bowing the strings

GREAT BIG STARS

sol   sol   sol   do¹

1. Great   big   stars   way   up__ yon - der,
2. Great   big   moon   way   up__ yon - der,

ACCOMPANIMENT
A supporting part for singers or instrumentalists

INTERVAL
The distance between two notes

Reba McEntire

Photo by George Holz

Reba McEntire

(b. 1955)

Reba McEntire was born in Oklahoma. She was discovered when she sang "The Star Spangled Banner" at the National Finals Rodeo. She is a country singer, motion picture and Broadway actress, television series star, author, and recording artist. Reba is a very successful female country artist with more than 50 million records sold!

The Banjo Lesson by Henry O. Tanner

- **What string instrument do you see in this painting?**

- **What are the man and boy doing?**

- **What do you think a banjo sounds like?**

Down in the Valley

KENTUCKY FOLK SONG

1. Down in the val - ley, the val - ley so
2. Roses love sun - shine, vio - lets love
3. Writing a let - ter con - tain - ing three

low.____ Hang your head o - ver, hear the wind
dew.____ An - gels in heav - en know I love
lines,____ ask - ing a ques - tion, will you be

blow.____ Hear the wind blow, dear, hear the wind
you.____ Know I love you, dear, know I love
mine?____ Will you be mine, dear, will you be

blow.____ Hang your head o - ver, hear the wind
you.____ An - gels in heav - en know I love
mine?____ Ask - ing a ques - tion, will you be

blow.____
you.____
mine?____

© 2003 BEAM ME UP MUSIC (ASCAP)   All Rights Administered by WARNER BROS. PUBLICATIONS U.S. INC.   All Rights Reserved

Will you be

Hill 'n Gully

CALYPSO FOLK SONG
Arranged by ROBERT W. SMITH

(A)

F   *sol sol sol la sol mi*   B♭ *do do do do*   F

Hill 'n gul-ly rid-er, hill 'n gul-ly.

sol sol sol la sol mi   B♭ *do do do do*   F   **B**

Hill 'n gul-ly rid-er, hill 'n gul-ly. { Rode my / And the

B♭   F

horse right down-town, hill 'n gul-ly. Wore a
peo-ple there say, hill 'n gul-ly. Give your

B♭   F

coat of dark brown, hill 'n gul-ly. } And my
horse some fresh hay, hill 'n gul-ly. }

© 2003 BEAM ME UP MUSIC (ASCAP)   All Rights Administered by WARNER BROS. PUBLICATIONS U.S. INC.   All Rights Reserved

face had an ug-ly frown, hill 'n gul-ly. 'Cause he

threw me and I tum-bled down, hill 'n gul-ly.

A

Hill 'n gul-ly rid-er, hill 'n gul-ly.

Last time shout: Hill 'n gully!

Hill 'n gul-ly rid-er, hill 'n gul-ly.

call-and-response

**A performance style or musical form in which
a leader's solo (the call) is followed by an answer
phrase performed by a group (the response).**

Cakewalk by Carmen Lomas Garza

- **Have you ever been to a cake-walk?**

- **How is music a part of a cake-walk?**

- **Are the people in the picture walking or dancing?**

mood

The way a composer, artist, or writer wants you to feel when you hear the music, see the art, or read the book or story

Golliwogg's Cake-walk

A (The A section begins after a short introduction.)

[musical notation]

[musical notation]

[musical notation]

[musical notation]

B This picture shows a variety of cakes.
Which cake would you like to eat?

Notice how the tempo of the music changes
throughout the B section of the piece.

A The A section repeats to end the piece
(with a slight rhythmic change in the last few measures).

Claude Debussy

Claude Debussy

(1862–1918)

Claude Debussy was born in France. He was a leader in writing music in a style called impressionism. It was called this because composers wanted to create a picture or feeling using sounds. His style was one of the most important influences on early twentieth-century music. He wrote for orchestra, ballet, piano, and opera. He called one piece for piano "Golliwogg's Cake-walk." One of his best-known compositions is probably "Clair de Lune."

Wake Me, Shake Me

AMERICAN FOLK SONG
Arranged by ROBERT W. SMITH

1. Wake me! Shake me!
2. Wake me! Shake me!
3. Wake me! Shake me!
4. Wake me! Shake me!

mi re do

Don't let me sleep too late. Got-ta
Don't let me sleep too late. Got-ta
Don't let me sleep too late. Got-ta
Don't let me sleep too late. Got-ta

get up bright and ear - ly in the morn-ing. Gon-na
wash my face in the morn-ing and
brush my shoes in the morn-ing and
sing my song in the morn-ing and

swing on the gar - den gate.
swing on the gar - den gate.
swing on the gar - den gate.
swing on the gar - den gate.

© 2003 BEAM ME UP MUSIC (ASCAP)   All Rights Administered by WARNER BROS. PUBLICATIONS U.S. INC.   All Rights Reserved

Scotland's Burning

TRADITIONAL ROUND
Arranged by ROBERT W. SMITH

Part I

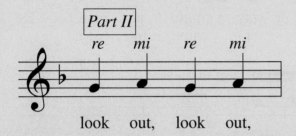

Scot-land's burn-ing, Scot-land's burn-ing,

Part II

look out, look out,

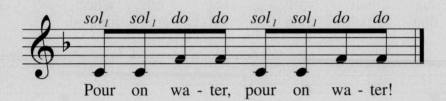

Fire! Fire! Fire! Fire!

Pour on wa-ter, pour on wa-ter!

© 2003 BEAM ME UP MUSIC (ASCAP)   All Rights Administered by WARNER BROS. PUBLICATIONS U.S. INC.   All Rights Reserved

Ostinato

Mallets

Pentatonic Scale

OLD DAN TUCKER

AMERICAN FOLK SONG
Arranged by ROBERT W. SMITH

Verse:

1. Old Dan Tuck-er was a might-y man. He
2. Old Dan Tuck-er came to town

washed his face in the fry-ing pan,
rid - ing a bil-ly goat, lead-ing a hound.

combed his hair with a wag - on wheel,
Hound dog barked, then bil-ly goat jumped;

had a tooth - ache in his heel. So}
Dan fell off and land-ed on a stump; so}

© 2003 BEAM ME UP MUSIC (ASCAP)   All Rights Administered by WARNER BROS. PUBLICATIONS U.S. INC.   All Rights Reserved

Refrain:

get out the way, old Dan Tuck - er,

get out the way, *sol₁ sol₁ la₁ do* old Dan Tuck - er.

Get out the way, old Dan Tuck - er,

you're too late to *sol₁ sol₁ la₁ do* get your sup - per.

Green Sally Up

AMERICAN FOLK TUNE
Arranged by MICHAEL STORY

(Gm)

f Green Sal - ly up, green Sal - ly down,
knee clap R clap knee clap L clap

green Sal - ly baked her 'pos - sum brown. I
knee clap R clap L clap both clap

asked my ma - ma for fif - ty cents to
knee clap R clap knee clap L clap

see the el - e - phant jump the fence. She
knee clap R clap L clap both clap

jumped so high, she touched the sky, and she
knee clap R clap knee clap L clap

did - n't come back 'til the fourth of Ju - ly. (Sing-in')
knee clap R clap L clap both clap

© 2003 BEAM ME UP MUSIC (ASCAP)   All Rights Administered by WARNER BROS. PUBLICATIONS U.S. INC.   All Rights Reserved

eighth notes

2-eight = ♫

J. AQUINO

149

RHYTHM	SYLLABLE	NAME
	= ta	= quarter note ("quart")
	= rest	= quarter rest ("rest")
	= ta-a	= half note ("half note")
	= ta-a-a	= dotted half note ("half note dot")
	= ta-a-a-a	= whole note ("whole note hold it")
	= ti-ti	= two eighth notes ("2-eight")
	= ti	= eighth note ("eight")
	= ti ta ti	= syncopation ("syncopa")

Seminole Duck Dance Song

SEMINOLE SONG
L.W. BALLARD

He hoh!   *mf* We   he - nuh   we he nah

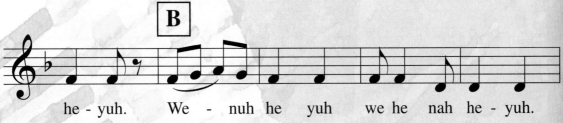

he - yuh.   We - nuh he   yuh   we he   nah he - yuh.

We - nuh he   yuh   we he   nah he - yuh.

© 2003 BEAM ME UP MUSIC (ASCAP)   All Rights Administered by WARNER BROS. PUBLICATIONS U.S. INC.   All Rights Reserved

Peace Like a River

TRADITIONAL
Arranged by ROBERT W. SMITH

1. I've got peace like a riv-er, I've got peace like a riv-er, I've got peace like a riv-er in my soul. I've got peace like a riv-er, I've got peace like a riv-er, I've got peace like a riv-er in my soul.

2. I've got love like the ocean,
I've got love like the ocean,
I've got love like the ocean in my soul.
I've got love like the ocean,
I've got love like the ocean,
I've got love like the ocean in my soul.

© 2003 BEAM ME UP MUSIC (ASCAP)   All Rights Administered by WARNER BROS. PUBLICATIONS U.S. INC.   All Rights Reserved

Rhythm	Syllable	Name

♩   = ta =   "quart"

♩ ♪   = ta-ti =   "quarter dot"   ♩.

♩ ♪ ♪ = ta-ti-ti = "quarter dot eight"   ♩. ♪

The dot adds one half the value of the note .

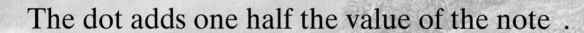

♪ ♪ ♪ = ♩ ♪ = ♩.

Tie means <u>plus</u>

♪ + ♪ + ♪ = ♩   + ♪ = ♩.

DOWN in the Ocean

By DEBBIE FAHMIE

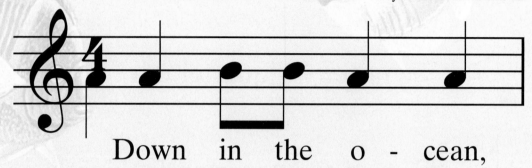

Down in the o - cean,

liv - ing in the sea.

Can you catch a big fish?

Not me!

156   © Debbie Fahmie   Used by Permission

rondo

A musical form in which the first section is repeated several times with a different section in between

Down in the Ocean

By DEBBIE FAHMIE

Down   in the o - cean,   liv - ing in the sea.

Can you catch a big   fish?   Not   me!

© Debbie Fahmie   Used by Permission

Down in the Ocean

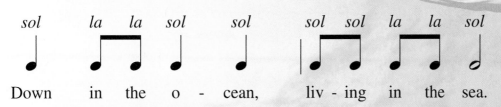

By DEBBIE FAHMIE

sol   *la*   *la*   *sol*   *sol*   *sol*   *sol*   *la*   *la*   *sol*

Down   in   the   o - cean,   liv - ing   in   the   sea.

sol   *sol*   *la*   *la*   *sol*   *sol*   *sol*   *do*

Can   you   catch   a   big   fish?   Not   me!

© Debbie Fahmie   Used by Permission

Eine Kleine Nachtmusik

("A Little Night Music" by Wolfgang Amadeus Mozart)

Follow this listening map as the string instruments play Wolfgang A. Mozart's exciting piece of night music. Focus on the melodic direction in the opening themes, and be sure to notice how the composer used dynamic contrast to make the piece exciting. Can you discover how many times these themes appear in the entire piece of music?

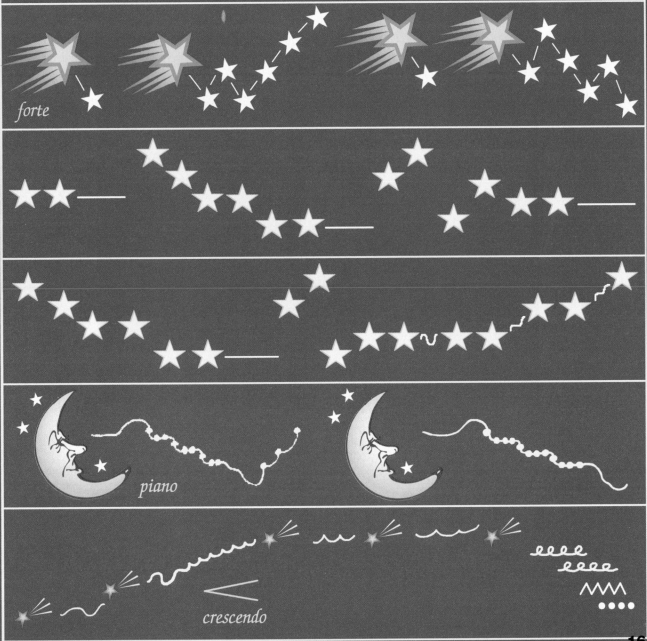

Wolfgang Amadeus Mozart

Wolfgang Amadeus Mozart

(1756–1791)

Wolfgang Amadeus Mozart was born in Austria. By the time he was eight years old, he was performing all over Europe for kings and queens. At the age of ten, he composed his first symphony, and at 11 he composed an opera. He had conducted 26 performances of his new opera before he was 15. Mozart composed hundreds of works for orchestra, piano, string quartet, voice, and other solo instruments and ensembles. One of his operas often performed is *The Magic Flute*.

OLD DAN TUCKER

AMERICAN FOLK SONG
Arranged by ROBERT W. SMITH

Verse:

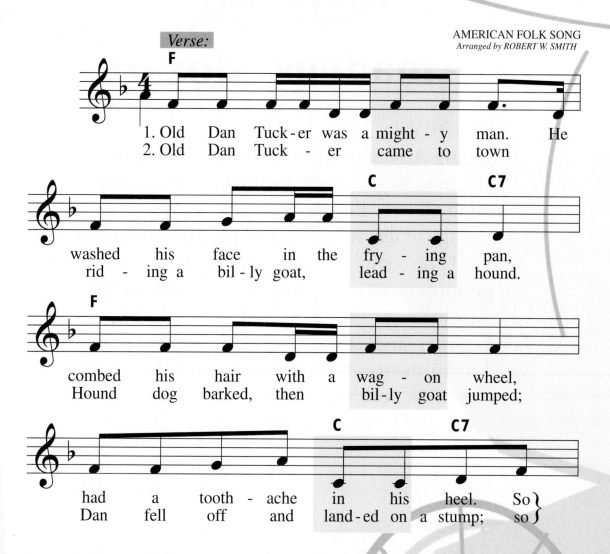

1. Old Dan Tuck-er was a might-y man. He
2. Old Dan Tuck-er came to town

washed his face in the fry-ing pan,
rid - ing a bil-ly goat, lead-ing a hound.

combed his hair with a wag-on wheel,
Hound dog barked, then bil-ly goat jumped;

had a tooth-ache in his heel. So }
Dan fell off and land-ed on a stump; so }

© 2003 BEAM ME UP MUSIC (ASCAP)   All Rights Administered by WARNER BROS. PUBLICATIONS U.S. INC.   All Rights Reserved

Are these steps, skips, or repeated patterns?

sol   la   sol

mi   re   do

Dave Brubeck

Image © Tony Stone Images, Stephen Johnson

Dave Brubeck

(b. 1920)

Dave Brubeck was born in Concord, California. The Dave Brubeck Quartet began traveling in Brubeck's station wagon, with the string bass tied to the roof. A composer and pianist, he is a jazz legend. Two of his well-known pieces are "Unsquare Dance" and "Blue Rondo à la Turk." "Take Five" was written by the quartet's saxophone player, Paul Desmond, but it is recognized as Dave Brubeck's theme song.

Blue Rondo à la Turk

rondo

A musical form in which the first section is repeated several times with a different section in between

solo

A performance by one person

♩ = Quarter Note = "Quart"

♫ = Eighth Notes = "2-eight"

Patriotic Medley

show good singing posture while standing

style

The special way something is done,
created, or performed

fiddle

hammered
dulcimer

banjo

tone color

The particular sound of an instrument or voice

tempo

The speed of the beat

dynamics

The loudness or softness of music

rhythm

Duration or length of time notes are sounded

melody

How pitches move up, down, or stay the same

Peace Like a River

setting
The location

John Williams

John Williams

(b. 1932)

John Williams was born in New York and later moved to Los Angeles. He served as the main conductor of the Boston Pops Orchestra from 1980 to 1993. As a composer, he is best known for scores from films such as *Star Wars*, *Raiders of the Lost Ark*, *E.T.*, *Jurassic Park*, the *Star Wars* sequels, *Superman*, *Home Alone*, and the *Harry Potter* movies.

Hill 'n Gully

Down in the Valley Two by Two

FOLK SONG
Arranged by ROBERT W. SMITH

F

1. Down in the val - ley, two by two,— my ba - by,

C ... **F**

two by two,— my ba - by, two by two.—

Down in the val - ley, two by two,— now—

C ... **F**

rise, Sal - ly, rise.—

2. Let me see you make a motion,
   Two by two, my baby,
   Two by two, my baby, two by two.
   Let me see you make a motion,
   Two by two, now rise, Sally, rise.

3. Let me see you make another one,
   Two by two, my baby,
   Two by two, my baby, two by two.
   Let me see you make another one,
   Two by two, now rise, Sally, rise.

4. Now choose somebody,
   Two by two, my baby,
   Two by two, my baby, two by two.
   Choose somebody,
   Two by two, now rise, Sally, rise. *Go!*

189

© 2003 BEAM ME UP MUSIC (ASCAP)   All Rights Administered by WARNER BROS. PUBLICATIONS U.S. INC.   All Rights Reserved

Seminole Duck Dance Song

SEMINOLE SONG
L.W. BALLARD

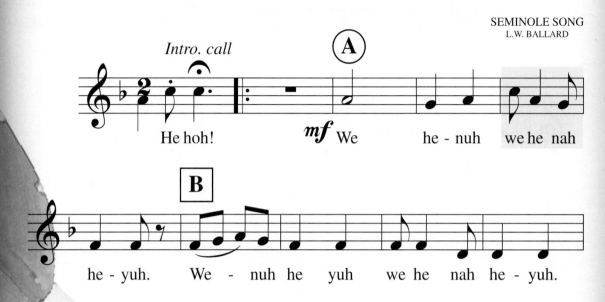

Intro. call

(A)

He hoh! *mf* We he - nuh we he nah

(B)

he - yuh. We - nuh he yuh we he nah he - yuh.

We - nuh he yuh we he nah he - yuh.

© 2003 BEAM ME UP MUSIC (ASCAP)   All Rights Administered by WARNER BROS. PUBLICATIONS U.S. INC.   All Rights Reserved

Down in the Valley Two by Two

FOLK SONG
Arranged by ROBERT W. SMITH

1. Down in the val-ley, two by two,— my ba-by,

two by two,— my ba-by, two by two.—

Down in the val-ley, two by two,— now—

rise, Sal-ly, rise.—

2. Let me see you make a motion,
   Two by two, my baby,
   Two by two, my baby, two by two.
   Let me see you make a motion,
   Two by two, now rise, Sally, rise.

3. Let me see you make another one,
   Two by two, my baby,
   Two by two, my baby, two by two.
   Let me see you make another one,
   Two by two, now rise, Sally, rise.

4. Now choose somebody,
   Two by two, my baby,
   Two by two, my baby, two by two.
   Choose somebody,
   Two by two, now rise, Sally, rise. *Go!*

Down in the Valley Two by Two

do   re   mi   sol   la

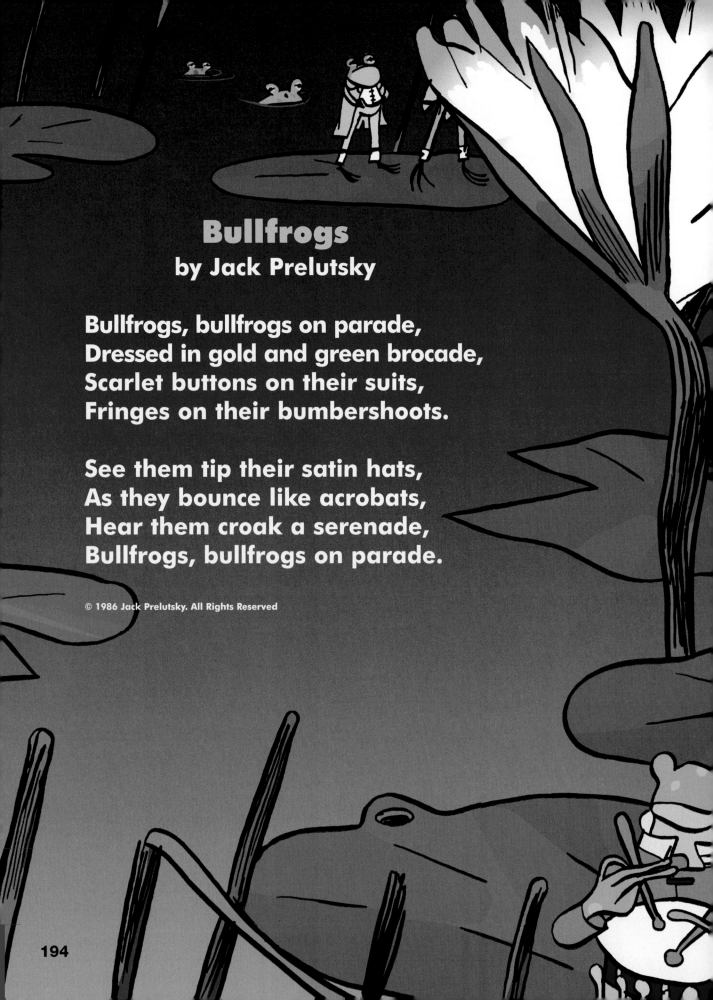

Bullfrogs
by Jack Prelutsky

Bullfrogs, bullfrogs on parade,
Dressed in gold and green brocade,
Scarlet buttons on their suits,
Fringes on their bumbershoots.

See them tip their satin hats,
As they bounce like acrobats,
Hear them croak a serenade,
Bullfrogs, bullfrogs on parade.

© 1986 Jack Prelutsky. All Rights Reserved

composed song

Music that is written by one or more persons

texture

The quality of a musical work that is determined by the number and types of its voices, instruments, melodies, and harmonies

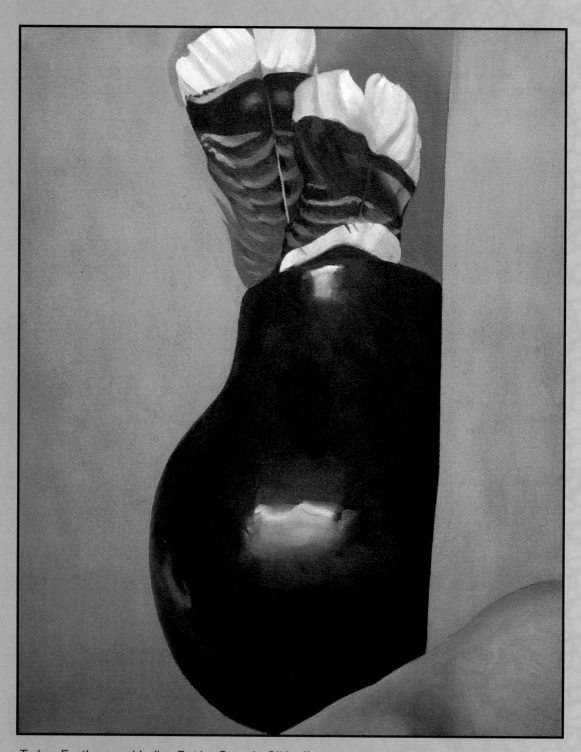

Turkey Feathers and Indian Pot by Georgia O'Keeffe

- **What do you see in this painting?**

- **How would the turkey feathers feel if you could touch them?**

- **How would the pot feel?**

- **Does this painting have texture?**

- **What gives it texture?**

Who am I?

Who am I?

Who am I?

Who am I?

violin

violin

A string instrument that is played by plucking (pizzicato) or bowing (arco)

Verse 1:
When I was a baby, a baby, a baby, when I was a baby,
well this what I do; I went goo, this a'way, goo,
that a'way, goo, this a'way. And that's what I do.

Verse 2:
When I went to school, to school, to school, when I went to school,
now this what I do; I went JUMP this a'way, JUMP that a'way,
JUMP this a'way. And that's what I do.

Verse 3:
When I was a teenager . . . I went unh . . .

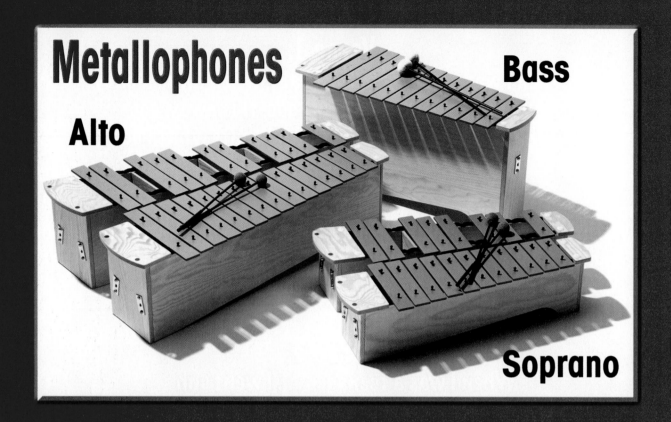

Metallophones

Alto

Bass

Soprano

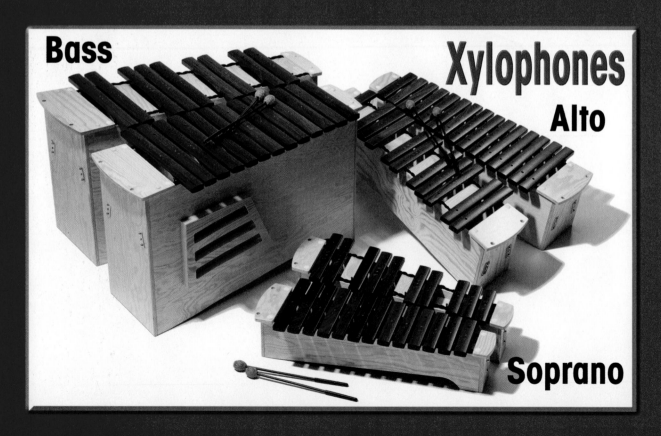

Bass

Xylophones

Alto

Soprano

Resonator Bells

Soprano Glockenspiel

pitched
Having highness
or lowness of sound

unpitched
Without highness
or lowness of sound

sound source
The origin of sound

double bass

**Sometimes called a bass viol or string bass—
the largest member of the string family**

VIOLIN   DOUBLE BASS

music criteria

**Standards by which music
and performance are evaluated**

cello

A four-string instrument of the string family that is held upright between the knees

VIOLIN   CELLO   DOUBLE BASS

Yo-Yo Ma

Yo-Yo Ma

(b. 1955)

Yo-Yo Ma was born in Paris, France, and later moved to the United States. He began his cello studies with his father at the age of four and gave his first public recital at the age of five. A ten-time Grammy® Award winner, Yo-Yo Ma has recorded more than 50 albums. He devotes time to work with young musicians in programs such as those at Interlochen and Tanglewood.

© John Lee/Star File

fiddle

banjo

mandolin

guitar

217

Violin, by Stradivari, Cremona, 1699

• **How would you describe the style of the picture *Violin*?**

• **What do you see in this picture?**

Celestial Quartet by Jim Stallings

- **What do you see in this painting?**

- **What is a quartet?**

- **Why is this painting called *Celestial Quartet*?**

- **What instruments are the musicians playing?**

- **How is the style of *Celestial Quartet* different from *Violin*?**

viola

A four-string musical instrument of the string family, slightly larger than a violin and having a deeper tone and a lower pitch

VIOLIN   **VIOLA**   **CELLO**   **DOUBLE BASS**

Cynthia Phelps

Photo: J. Henry Fair

Cynthia Phelps

(b. 1960)

Cynthia Phelps is a native of the United States and lives mostly in California and New York. She grew up in a family of musicians—all of whom were born with perfect pitch. Cynthia started playing the viola when she was four. She says, "When I picked up my first viola, I felt like I had found my voice—this was the voice I heard in my head." In addition to being principal violist of the New York Philharmonic orchestra and a recording artist, Cynthia Phelps has performed throughout the world as a soloist with orchestras.

Bullfrogs Rondo

You Are My Sunshine

(Bluegrass Style)

Words and Music by
JIMMIE DAVIS and CHARLES MITCHELL
Arranged by ROBERT W. SMITH

You are my sun - shine,____ my on - ly

sun - shine.____ You make me hap - py____ when skies are

gray._____ You'll nev - er know, dear,____ how much I

love you. Please don't take my sun - shine a - way.

© 1940 PEER INTERNATIONAL CORPORATION
Copyright Renewed   All Rights Reserved   Used by Permission

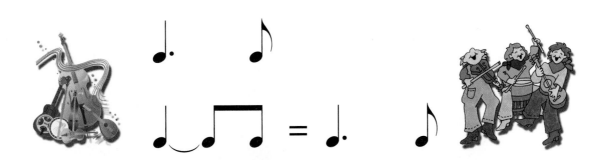

Fancy Dancing

By JUNE HINCKLEY
Arranged by ROBERT W. SMITH

sol₁ la₁ ti₁   A♭   do

Just keep a stea-dy beat, and move your

par-ty feet. It's so much fun to be fan-cy

E♭   ti₁   A♭

danc - ing. No mat-ter how you move, just get in -

to the groove. We're gon-na shine with our fan-cy

© 2003 BEAM ME UP MUSIC (ASCAP)   All Rights Administered by WARNER BROS. PUBLICATIONS U.S. INC.   All Rights Reserved

danc - ing.   Just move   your heel   and toe.

Don't be   a - fraid to go. 'Cause ev - 'ry - one   is   danc - ing.

Now move   your hips and knees. Shake like   you're in   a breeze.

Now ev - 'ry - one   is   danc - ing.

Photograph of Maurice (left) and Gregory (right) Hines

- **What kind of dance are the Hines brothers doing?**

- **How can you tell?**

- **Could they perform this style of dance to "Fancy Dancing"?**

- **Why or why not?**

- One of the members of our orchestral string family is missing. Which is it?

- Which instrument is used twice in the string quartet?

String quartet in Catherine Palace in Pushkin, Russia

235

"Spring" from *The Four Seasons* by *Antonio Vivaldi*

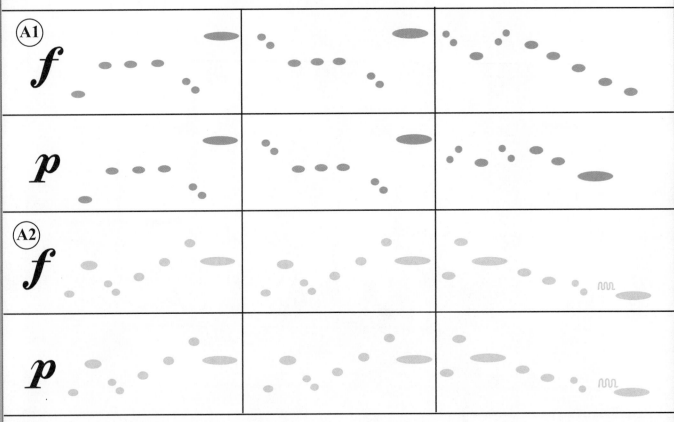

Listen to the "conversation" between the violins.

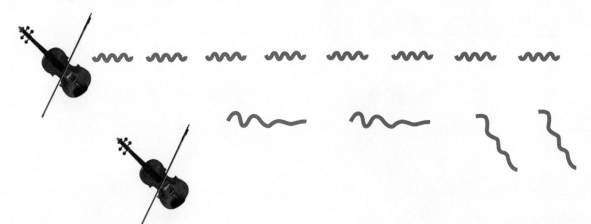

The conversation continues...

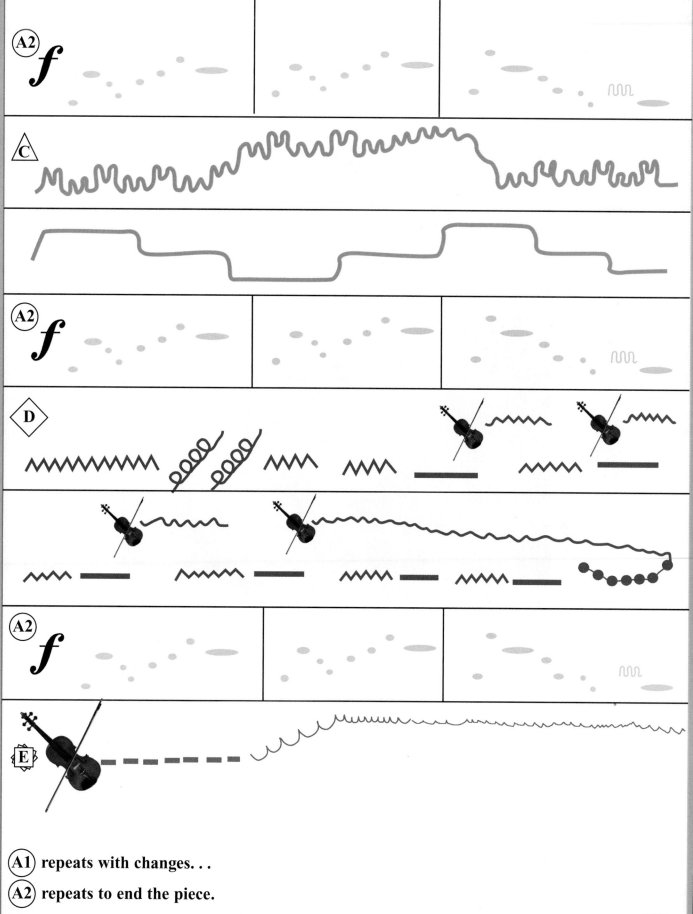

A1 repeats with changes. . .

A2 repeats to end the piece.

Antonio Vivaldi

Antonio Vivaldi

(1678–1741)

Antonio Vivaldi was born in Italy and lived in Venice, Mantua, Rome, and Prague. He became an ordained priest probably because this was the only way for a poor family to receive free schooling. Vivaldi spent most of his working life as a violin teacher. He wrote many concertos—works for one or more solo instruments and orchestra—such as *The Four Seasons*.

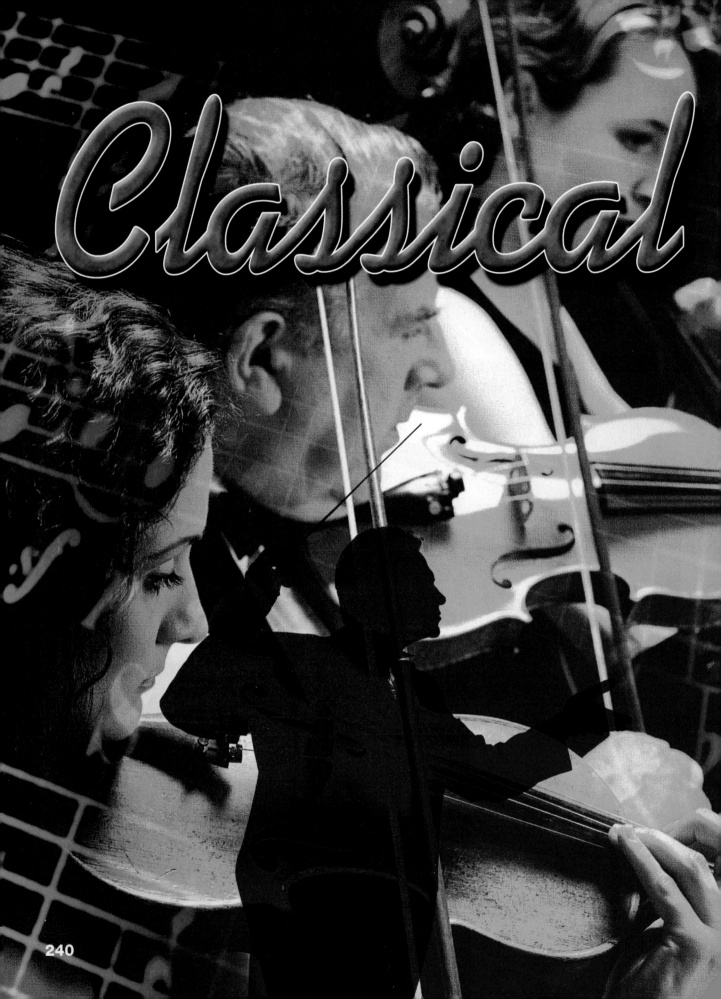

Classical

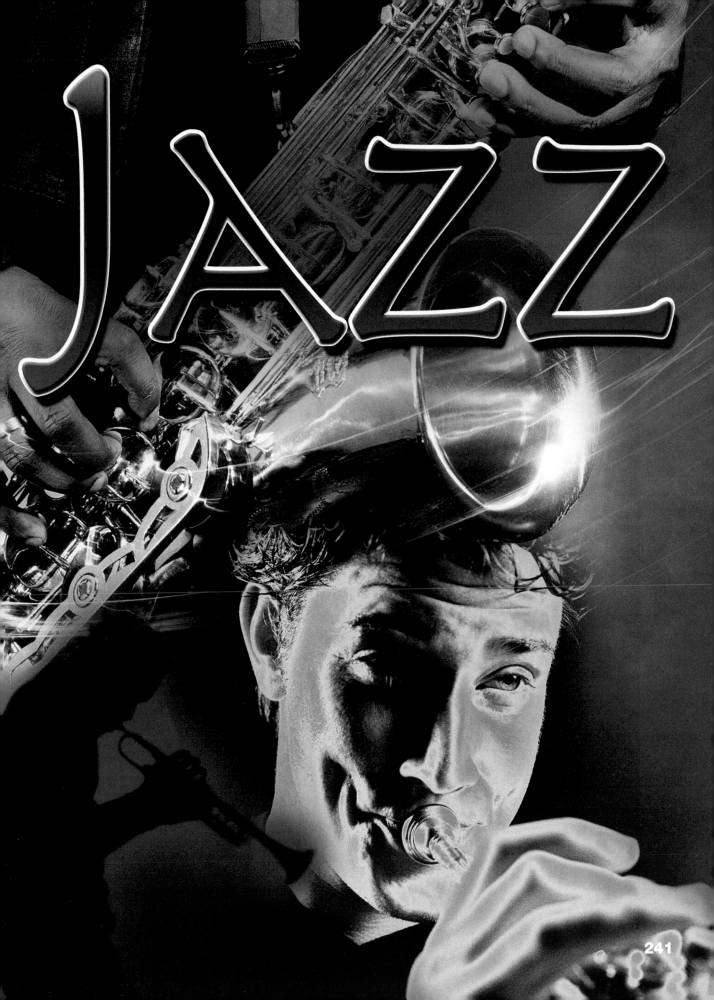

JAZZ

Yehudi Menuhin

Stephane Grappelli

Ray Brown

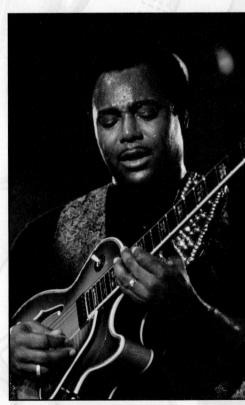
George Benson

Yehudi Menuhin

(1916–1999)

Yehudi Menuhin was an American musician who lived in New York, Paris, Venice, and Germany. He was a teacher, conductor, and composer. His performances on violin and viola began impressing audiences when he was only seven years old. At his Berlin concert when he was 13, Menuhin's performance inspired Albert Einstein to say: "Now I know there is a God in heaven!"

Stephane Grappelli

(1908–1997)

Stephane Grappelli was born in France and lived in Paris, where he eventually became a jazz violinist. At the end of World War I, Grappelli helped his father pay the bills by working as a pianist, accompanying silent films in a cinema. Grappelli's father gave him a second-hand violin and taught him the scales when he was 13. He formed the Hot Club of France quintet.

Ray Brown

(1926–2002)

Ray Brown was born in Pittsburgh, Pennsylvania. His musical education began with piano lessons, but he switched to the bass to be in the school orchestra. In New York, he joined Snookum Russell's band. Ray became famous as a young bassist on the tune "One Bass Hit" with the Dizzy Gillespie Orchestra, a bebop big band.

George Benson

(b. 1943)

George Benson was born in Pittsburgh, Pennsylvania. He first sang as a pro when he was only eight years old. Benson is a composer, improviser, guitarist, and singer in many styles, including hard bop, rock 'n' roll, and R&B.

The Star Spangled Banner

Words by FRANCIS SCOTT KEY
Arranged by ROBERT W. SMITH

© 2003 BEAM ME UP MUSIC (ASCAP)   All Rights Administered by WARNER BROS. PUBLICATIONS U.S. INC.   All Rights Reserved

Three Flags by Jasper Johns

- How many flags do you see in this picture?

- There are 50 states in the United States. Count the number of stars in the smallest flag in *Three Flags*. How many are there? Why?

- What songs about the American flag do you know?

Ouma
(Mother Horse and Colt)

Words by RYUSHA HAYASHI
Music by TSUNE MATSUSHIMA
Arranged by ROBERT W. SMITH

O - u - ma - no   o - ya - ko - wa

na - ka - yo - shi - ko - yo - shi;   i - tsu - de - mo -

i   sho - ni   Po - ku-ri, Po - ku-ri,   A - ru - ku.

O - u - ma - no   ka - a - sa - a   ya - sa - shi - i   ka - a - san:

Ko - u - ma - wo   mi - na   ga - ra   Po - ku-ri, Po - ku-ri,

A - ru - ku.   Po - ku-ri, Po - ku-ri,   A - ru - ku.

© 2003 BEAM ME UP MUSIC (ASCAP)   All Rights Administered by WARNER BROS. PUBLICATIONS U.S. INC.   All Rights Reserved

Sitar

India

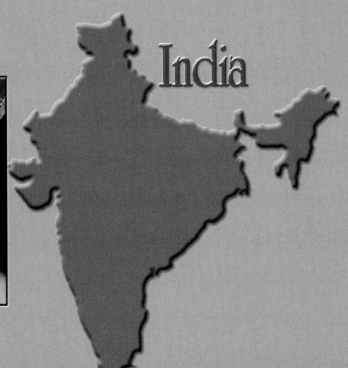

Welsh Harp

Wales

Strings of the World

China

Pipa

Vietnam

Dàn Bâù

Koto

Japan

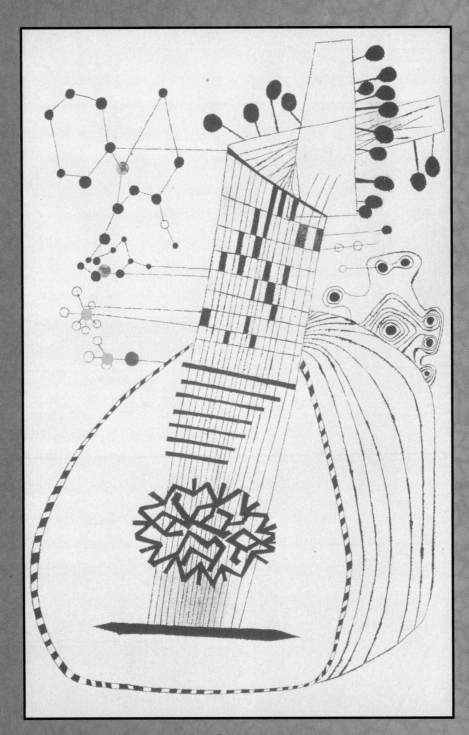

Lute and Molecule No. 2 by Ben Shahn

- **This is a drawing of a string instrument we have not heard.**

- **What is the instrument called?**

- **How do you know?**

- **What do you see in this drawing?**

- **Do you like this artwork? Why or why not?**

Koto

Minoru Miki

Minoru Miki

(b. 1930)

Minoru Miki was born in Tokushima, Japan. In 1969 Miki and Keiko Nosaka invented the 20-string koto, which later had 21 strings. His album, *The Music of Minoru Miki*, took the Grand Prize in Japan's 1970 National Arts Festival. In 1993, Miki became the artistic director of Orchestra Asia (ORA), a group that combines Japanese, Chinese, and Korean instruments.

JAPAN

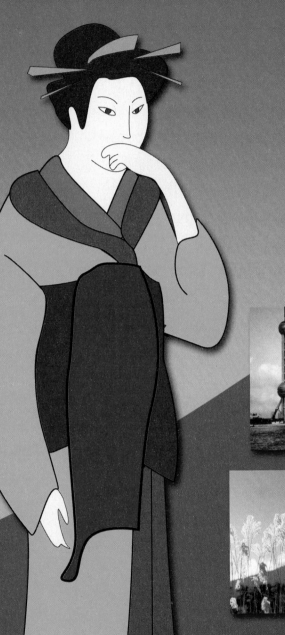

Deta, Deta

(The Moon)

JAPANESE CHILDREN'S SONG
Collected and Transcribed by
KATHY B. SORENSEN

F

	sol	*mi*	*sol*	*mi*	*do*	*re*
Japanese:	De	ta	de	ta	tsu	ki
Phonetic Pronunciation:	Day	tah	day	tah	tsoo	kee
English:	*Now*	*the*	*moon*	*is*	*com*	*- ing*

mi		*sol*	*la*	*sol*	*mi*	*sol*	*la*	*sol*
ga.		Ma___	ru	i	ma___	ru,		
gah.		Mah - ah	loo	ee	mah - ah	loo		
out!		*Big*	*and*	*round,*	*so*	*big*	*and round,*	

mi	*sol*	*la*	*sol*	*mi*	*re*		*do*	*re*	*mi*	*la*
i	ma	n	ma	ru	i.		Bo___	n	no	
ee	mah	n	mah	loo	ee.		Boh	on	noh yoh -	
as	*round___*	*as*	*a*	*tray.*			*Big___*	*and___*		

(chords: **C** ... **F**)

sol	*mi*		*re*	*mi*		*do*	
yo	na		tsu	ki		ga.	
oh	nah		tsoo	kee		gah.	
round	*just*		*like*	*a*		*tray.*	

(chords: **C** ... **F**)

2. Now the moon is hiding!
   Gone away, oh gone away,
   Behind the clouds.
   Black as ink, behind the clouds.

© 1991 Kathy B. Sorensen   © 2003 Kathy B. Sorensen   All Rights Reserved   Used by Permission

Kabuki
Theatre
Players

Japanese Tea Ceremony

Koto

Haiku

A gi-ant fire fly:
that way, this way, that way, this
and it pass-es by.

Issa, 1763–1784

Well, let's go
Up to the place
Where we'll fall down and look at the snow!

Basho, 1644–1694

**On the tem-ple bell
Set-tles and is sleep-ing
A but-ter-fly.**

Buson, 1716–1784

**One per-son
And one fly
In the big wait-ing room.**

Issa, 1763–1823

**With what voice,
And what song would you sing, spi-der,
In this au-tumn breeze?**

Basho, 1644–1694

Mochibana by Keiko Kodai

- **How can you tell this is a Japanese painting?**

- **Can you find:**
  - **Cherry blossoms**
  - **A rabbit**
  - **A candlestick**
  - **Two dresses**
  - **A top**

- **What else can you find in this painting?**

- **Can you find any lines that look like phrases?**

- **How do you know this is a painting about spring?**

music criteria
The tone color matches
the mood of the haiku.

266

Perform your haiku soundscape.

What would you change?

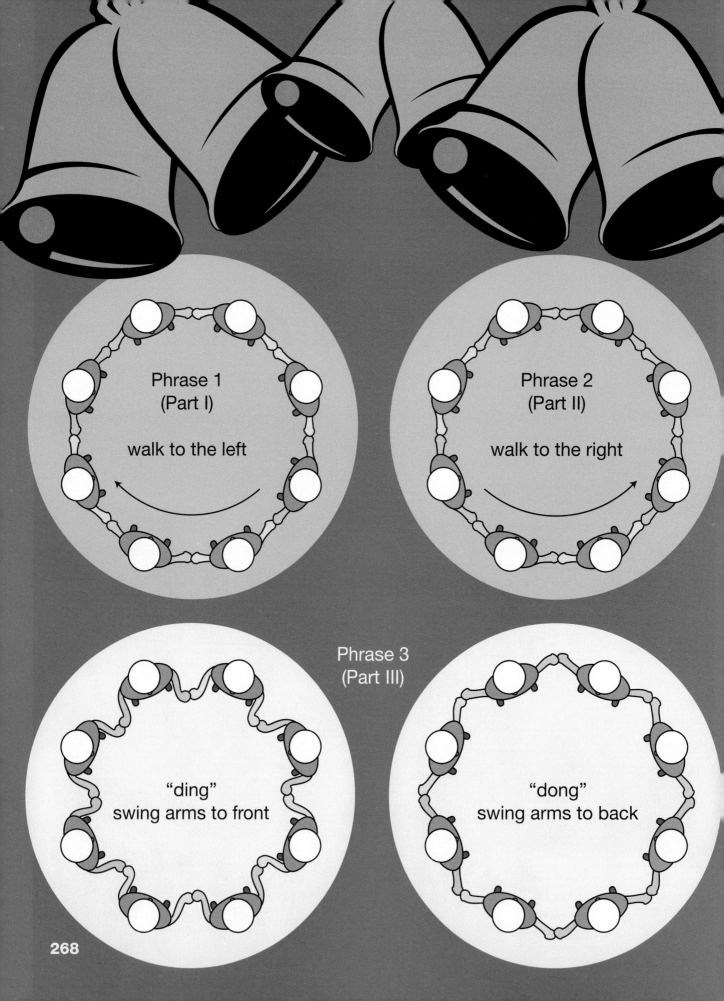

Phrase 1
(Part I)

walk to the left

Phrase 2
(Part II)

walk to the right

Phrase 3
(Part III)

"ding"
swing arms to front

"dong"
swing arms to back

268

Oh, How Lovely Is the Evening

TRADITIONAL GERMAN MELODY
Arranged by JACK BULLOCK

Part I

Oh, how love - ly is the

mi re do *mi re do*

eve - ning, is the eve - ning.

Part II

When the bells are sweet - ly ring - ing,

Part III

sweet - ly ring - ing. Ding, dong,

ding, dong, ding, dong.

(Final phrase)

Ding, dong, ding.

© 2003 BEAM ME UP MUSIC (ASCAP)   All Rights Administered by WARNER BROS. PUBLICATIONS U.S. INC.   All Rights Reserved

Ostinato

Mallets

Sky and Water I by M. C. Escher

- Why do you think the artist called this artwork *Sky and Water*?

- How many birds and fish do you see?

- How are the fish in this artwork different from each other?

- Are there patterns in this artwork? Where?

Canoe Song
(Canon)

CAMP ROUND
Arranged by MICHAEL STORY

My pad - dle's keen and bright,

flash-ing with sil - ver. Fol-low the wild goose flight,

dip, dip, and swing.

© 2003 BEAM ME UP MUSIC (ASCAP)   All Rights Administered by WARNER BROS. PUBLICATIONS U.S. INC.   All Rights Reserved

Ostinato

canon

A musical form in which the same music or movement is performed by two or more persons beginning at different times so they overlap

272

Hill 'n Gully

CALYPSO FOLK SONG
Arranged by ROBERT W. SMITH

Verse 1:

Hill 'n gul - ly rid - er, hill 'n gul - ly.

Hill 'n gul - ly rid - er, hill 'n gul - ly. Rode my

horse right down - town, hill 'n gul - ly. Wore a

coat of dark brown, hill 'n gul - ly. And my

face had an ug - ly frown, hill 'n gul - ly. 'Cause he

threw me and I tum - bled down, hill 'n gul - ly.

Hill 'n gul - ly rid - er, hill 'n gul - ly.

Hill 'n gul - ly rid - er, hill 'n gul - ly.

Interlude:

Verse 2:

Hill 'n gul - ly rid - er,   hill 'n   gul - ly.

Hill 'n gul - ly rid - er,   hill 'n   gul - ly.   And the

peo - ple   there   say,   hill 'n   gul - ly.   Give your

horse   some   fresh   hay,   hill 'n   gul - ly.   And my

face   had an   ug - ly frown,   hill 'n   gul - ly.   'Cause he

threw   me   and   I   tum - bled down,   hill 'n   gul - ly.

Hill 'n gul - ly rid - er,   hill 'n   gul - ly.

Last time shout: Hill 'n gully!

Hill 'n gul - ly rid - er,   hill 'n   gul - ly.

Rhythm	Syllables	Name
o	= ta-a-a-a (sound) =	whole note
		(whole note hold it)
▬	= ta-a-a-a (silent) =	whole rest

whole rest

A rest containing four beats of silence (in $\frac{4}{4}$)

Long-Legged Sailor

Adapted and Arranged by
MICHAEL STORY

Have you ev-er, ev-er, ev-er in your

{ long -
{ short -
{ bow -
} leg-ged life met a { long -
{ short
{ bow
} leg-ged sail-or with a

{ long -
{ short -
{ bow -
} leg-ged wife? No, I nev-er, nev-er, nev-er in my

{ long -
{ short -
{ bow -
} leg-ged life met a { long -
{ short -
{ bow -
} leg-ged sail-or with a

{ long -
{ short -
{ bow -
} leg-ged wife.

© 2003 BEAM ME UP MUSIC (ASCAP)   All Rights Administered by WARNER BROS. PUBLICATIONS U.S. INC.   All Rights Reserved

ti₁   *do*

Morton Gould

Morton Gould

(1913–1996)

Morton Gould was born in Richmond Hill, New York. As a child he was identified as a talented composer and improviser. He would also become a conductor and pianist. As a teenager, he worked in New York's vaudeville and movie theaters. Gould was the first staff pianist at Radio City Music Hall. Gould has said, "Composing is my lifeblood." His composing has won him a Pulitzer Prize and *Musical America*'s 1994 Composer-of-the-Year award. Gould is known as a skilled composer, conductor, and performer.

Canoe Song

♪ = ti = eighth note (eight)

♩ = ta = quarter note (quart)

♪♩♪ = ti-ta-ti = eighth quarter eighth (syncopa)

♩ = ta-a = half note (half note)

𝅝 = ta-a-a-a = whole note (whole note hold it)

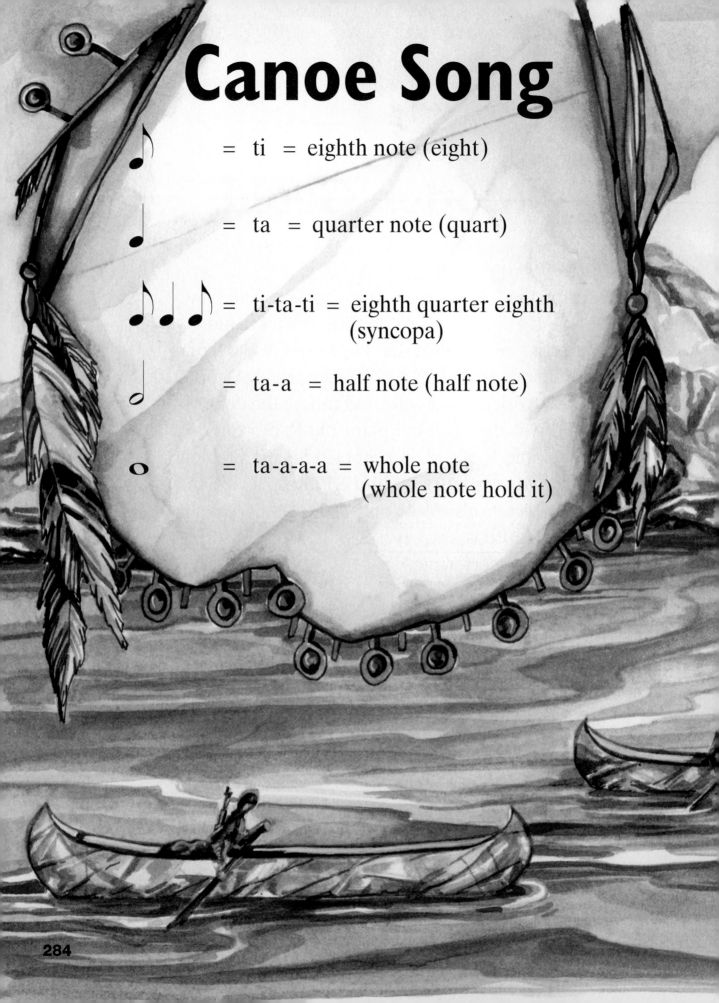

Eggs Encircled by Carlotta M. Corpron

- **What do you see in this artwork?**

- **We have been studying canons in music. Does this artwork show canons?**

- **Where are the canons in this artwork?**

- **Is this a drawing, painting, sculpture, or photograph?**

- **How can you tell?**

- **Have you ever taken a photograph?**

- **What did you photograph?**

Listen to the Mockingbird

Verse:

TRADITIONAL
Arranged by JACK BULLOCK

© 2003 BEAM ME UP MUSIC (ASCAP) All Rights Administered by WARNER BROS. PUBLICATIONS U.S. INC. All Rights Reserved

♩ = ta = quarter note (quart)

♫ = ti-ti = eighth notes (2-eight)

♬ = ti-ki-ti-ki = sixteenth notes (sixteen sixteen)

A Ram Sam Sam

MOROCCAN SONG
Arranged by ROBERT W. SMITH

A ram sam sam, a ram sam sam, gu-li gu-li gu-li gu-li gu-li, ram sam sam. A ra - fi, a ra - fi, gu-li gu-li gu-li gu-li gu-li, ram sam sam.

© 2003 BEAM ME UP MUSIC (ASCAP)   All Rights Administered by WARNER BROS. PUBLICATIONS U.S. INC.   All Rights Reserved

Long-Legged Sailor

Adapted and Arranged by
MICHAEL STORY

© 2003 BEAM ME UP MUSIC (ASCAP)   All Rights Administered by WARNER BROS. PUBLICATIONS U.S. INC.   All Rights Reserved

Long-Legged Sailor

Verse 1 and Verse 3:

Adapted and Arranged by
MICHAEL STORY

© 2003 BEAM ME UP MUSIC (ASCAP)   All Rights Administered by WARNER BROS. PUBLICTIONS U.S. INC.   All Rights Reserved

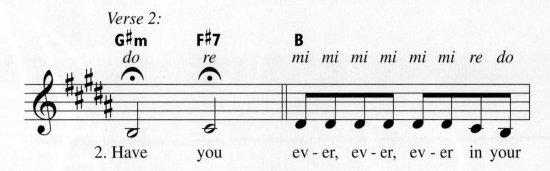

Verse 2:

G♯m   F♯7   B

do   re   mi mi mi mi mi mi re do

2. Have   you   ev - er, ev - er, ev - er in your

                                    G♯m

mi   mi mi mi   do re   mi   mi mi mi mi re do

short - leg-ged life   met a   short - leg-ged sail - or with a

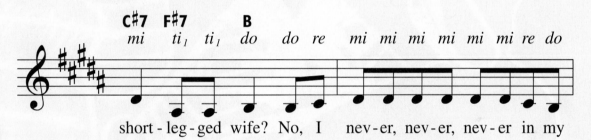

C♯7 F♯7   B

mi   ti₁ ti₁ do   do re   mi mi mi mi mi mi re do

short - leg - ged wife? No, I   nev - er, nev - er, nev - er in my

                                    G♯m

mi   mi mi mi   do re   mi   mi mi mi mi re do

short - leg-ged life   met a   short - leg-ged sail - or with a

C♯7   F♯7   B

mi   ti₁   ti₁   do

short - leg - ged wife.

sixteenth note

Old Brass Wagon

WESTERN FOLK SONG
Arranged by ROBERT W. SMITH

1. Cir - cle to the left, old brass wag - on.
2. Skip-ping all a - round, old brass wag - on.

Cir - cle to the left, old brass wag - on.
Skip-ping all a - round, old brass wag - on.

Cir - cle to the left, old brass wag - on,
Skip-ping all a - round, old brass wag - on,

you're the one, my dar - ling.
you're the one, my dar - ling. } Swing, oh swing, old brass wag-on.

Swing, oh swing, old brass wag-on. Swing, oh swing, old brass wag-on,

Last time: Yee-haw!

you're the one, my dar - ling.

© 2003 BEAM ME UP MUSIC (ASCAP)   All Rights Administered by WARNER BROS. PUBLICATIONS U.S. INC.   All Rights Reserved

Benjamin Britten

Benjamin Britten

(1913–1976)

Benjamin Britten was born in England. He was the youngest of four children, and his father was a dentist. Britten studied piano and viola as a child. He grew up to be a writer of operas such as *A Midsummer Night's Dream,* operettas such as *Paul Bunyan,* orchestra pieces such as *The Young Person's Guide to the Orchestra,* and choral works such as *A Ceremony of Carols.*

Johann Sebastian Bach

Johann Sebastian Bach

(1685–1750)

Johann Sebastian Bach was born in Germany to an important family of musicians and composers. At the age of ten, he became an orphan and went to live with his older brother, Johann Christoph. This brother was the organist at St. Michael's Church, and he gave J. S. keyboard lessons. J. S. later became a court musician and composer and then became director of music. Bach was married two times and had 20 children (seven with Maria and 13 with Anna). Several of his children also became celebrated musicians. J. S. Bach is considered one of the greatest composers in history. Some of his compositions include *The Brandenberg Concertos*; *The Well-Tempered Clavier*; *Jesu, Joy of Man's Desiring*; and *The Art of the Fugue*.

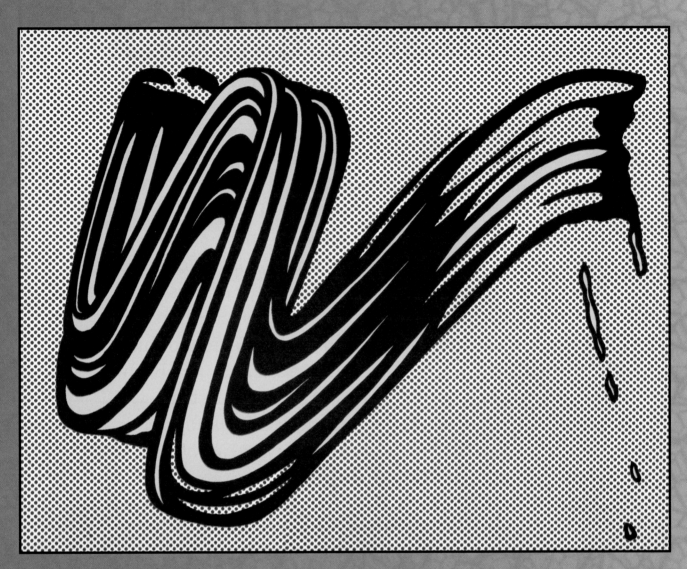

Brushstroke by Roy Lichtenstein

- Do you see any canons in this artwork? Where?

- Are there any phrases? Where?

- Do you like this artwork? Why or why not?

- What kind of a brush could create this stroke?

Choose a Canon

Oh, How Lovely Is the Evening

Canoe Song

Sweetly Sings the Donkey

Star Light, Star Bright

Make New Friends

Scotland's Burning

MaryAnn Elizabeth

A Ram Sam Sam

OLD DAN TUCKER

AMERICAN FOLK SONG
Arranged by ROBERT W. SMITH

Verse:

1. Old Dan Tuck-er was a might-y man. He
2. Old Dan Tuck-er came to town

washed his face in the fry-ing pan,
rid-ing a bil-ly goat, lead-ing a hound.

combed his hair with a wag-on wheel,
Hound dog barked, then bil-ly goat jumped;

had a tooth-ache in his heel. So
Dan fell off and land-ed on a stump; so

© 2003 BEAM ME UP MUSIC (ASCAP) All Rights Administered by WARNER BROS. PUBLICATIONS U.S. INC. All Rights Reserved

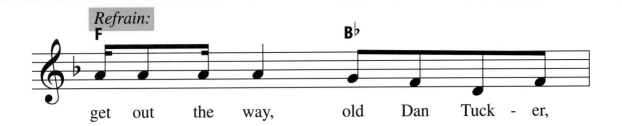

get out the way, old Dan Tuck - er,

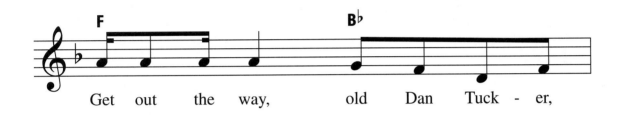

get out the way, old Dan Tuck - er.

Get out the way, old Dan Tuck - er,

you're too late to get your sup - per.

Peace Like a River

TRADITIONAL
Arranged by ROBERT W. SMITH

2. I've got love like the ocean,
   I've got love like the ocean,
   I've got love like the ocean in my soul.
   I've got love like the ocean,
   I've got love like the ocean,
   I've got love like the ocean in my soul.

© 2003 BEAM ME UP MUSIC (ASCAP)   All Rights Administered by WARNER BROS. PUBLICATIONS U.S. INC.   All Rights Reserved

Hill 'n Gully

CALYPSO FOLK SONG
Arranged by ROBERT W. SMITH

A

sol sol sol la sol mi   do do   do do

Hill 'n gul-ly rid-er, hill 'n gul-ly.

sol sol sol la sol mi   do do   do do

B

Hill 'n gul-ly rid-er, hill 'n gul-ly. { Rode my
And the

horse right down-town, hill 'n gul-ly. Wore a
peo-ple there say, hill 'n gul-ly. Give your

coat of dark brown, hill 'n gul-ly.} And my
horse some fresh hay, hill 'n gul-ly.}

© 2003 BEAM ME UP MUSIC (ASCAP)   All Rights Administered by WARNER BROS. PUBLICATIONS U.S. INC.   All Rights Reserved

face had an ug - ly frown, hill 'n gul - ly. 'Cause he

threw me and I tum - bled down, hill 'n gul - ly.

A Hill 'n gul - ly rid - er, hill 'n gul - ly.

Last time shout: Hill 'n gully!

Hill 'n gul - ly rid - er, hill 'n gul - ly.

All the Pretty Little Horses

All the Pretty Little Horses

© 2003 BEAM ME UP MUSIC (ASCAP)   All Rights Administered by WARNER BROS. PUBLICATIONS U.S. INC.   All Rights Reserved

This Land Is Your Land

Words and Music by
WOODY GUTHRIE
Arranged by MICHAEL STORY

Refrain:

This land is your land,____ this land is my land,____ from Cal - i - for - nia____ to the New York Is - land;____ from the red - wood for - est____ to the Gulf Stream wa - ters;____ this land was made for you and me.

To Verse
End here last time

TRO – © 1956, 1958, 1970 and 1972 LUDLOW MUSIC, INC., New York, NY   Copyrights Renewed   All Rights Reserved   Used by Permission

Verse:

C

As I was walk - ing_____ that rib-bon of

G   D

high - way,_____ I saw a - bove me_____

G

_ that end - less sky - way,_____ I saw be -

C   G

low me_____ that gold - en val - ley,_____

To Refrain

D   G

this land was made for you and me.

317

Oh, How Lovely Is the Evening

Look at the time signature of this piece.

Is this song in duple or triple?

How do you know?

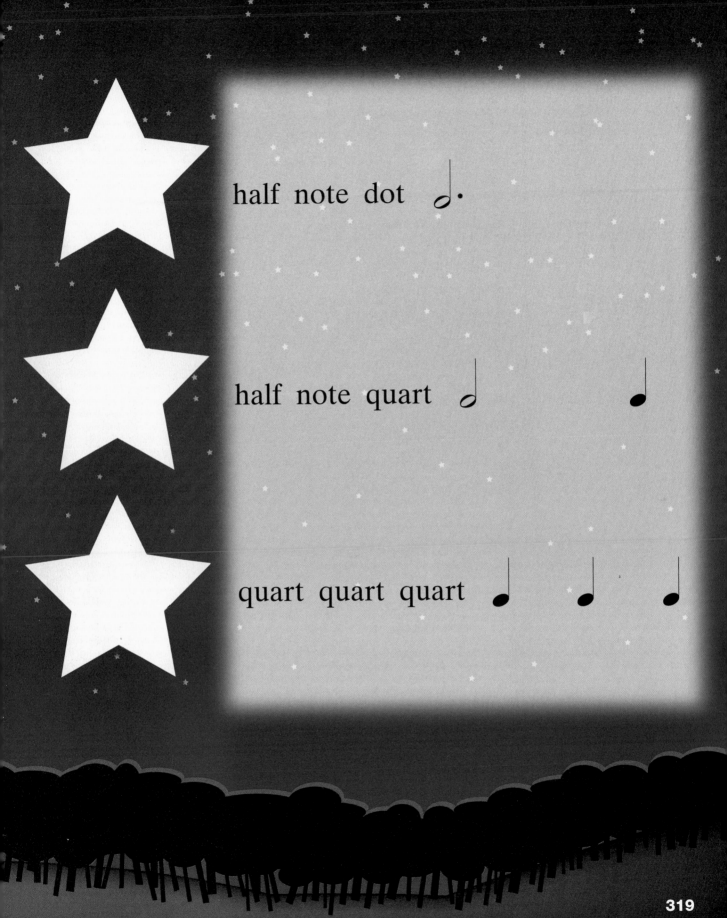

half note dot

half note quart

quart quart quart

Great Big Stars

Slowly

AFRICAN-AMERICAN SPIRITUAL
Arranged by MICHAEL STORY

1. Great big stars way up yonder,
2. Great big moon way up yonder,

great big stars way up yonder,
great big moon way up yonder,

great big stars way up yonder,
great big moon way up yonder,

oh, my lit - tle soul's gon - na shine, shine.

Oh, my lit - tle soul's gon - na shine, shine.

Oh, my lit - tle soul's gon - na shine, shine.

Oh, my lit - tle soul's gon - na shine, shine.

© 2003 BEAM ME UP MUSIC (ASCAP)   All Rights Administered by WARNER BROS. PUBLICATIONS U.S. INC.   All Rights Reserved

duple
Set of two

triple
Set of three

Find the duple and triple patterns

Scotland's Burning

TRADITIONAL ROUND
Arranged by ROBERT W. SMITH

Part I

sol₁ sol₁ do do sol₁ sol₁ do do

Scot-land's burn-ing, Scot-land's burn-ing,

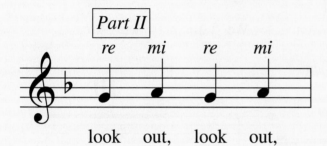

Part II

re mi re mi

look out, look out,

sol sol sol sol

Fire! Fire! Fire! Fire!

sol₁ sol₁ do do sol₁ sol₁ do do

Pour on wa-ter, pour on wa-ter!

© 2003 BEAM ME UP MUSIC (ASCAP)   All Rights Administered by WARNER BROS. PUBLICATIONS U.S. INC.   All Rights Reserved

Ostinato

Mallets

Children of the World

Children's Chorus
Gently

Keyboard chords → E♭

By BRANDON BARNES
and ROBERT W. SMITH

(Wait for your teacher to show you when to sing.)

We are,__ we are,__

we are__ the chil-dren.__ We are,__ we are,__

we are__ the chil-dren.__

(Wait for your teacher to show you when to sing.)

We are__ the chil-dren,__ chil-dren of__ the world.

We are__ the chil-dren,__ chil-dren of__ the world.

We are,__ we are,__ we are__ the chil-dren.__

© 2003 BEAM ME UP MUSIC (ASCAP)   All Rights Administered by WARNER BROS. PUBLICATIONS U.S. INC.   All Rights Reserved

We are,___ we are,___ we are___ the chil - dren.___

Driving!

(Wait for your teacher to show you when to sing.)

We are,___ we are,___

we are___ the chil - dren.___ We are,___ we are,___

Soaring!

we are___ the chil - dren.___ We are___ the chil - dren,___

chil - dren of___ the world. We are___ the chil - dren,___

chil - dren of___ the world. We are___ the chil - dren,___

chil - dren of the world!_____

Photography: Donald Norsworthy

Goodbye

Glossary

AB form	A musical form consisting of two different sections (page 83)
accompaniment	A supporting part for singers or instrumentalists (page 127)
arco	To play a string instrument with a bow rather than by plucking (page 125)
audience	A group of people who listen to or watch a live performance
audience etiquette	The rules for proper behavior during a live performance (page 102)
ballad	A song that tells a story (page 106)
band	A large group of musicians who play wind and percussion instruments together (no string instruments) (page 95)
bluegrass	A style of music that originated in the southern United States that contains rapid tempos, jazz-like improvisation, and emphasis on string instruments such as the banjo and guitar
body percussion	Sounds that are produced by actions such as clapping, snapping, and stomping (page 47)
call-and-response	A performance style or musical form in which a leader's solo (the call) is followed by an answer phrase performed by a group (the response) (page 135)
canon	A musical form in which the same music or movement is performed by two or more persons beginning at different times so they overlap (page 272)
chant	A text recited in rhythm
chord	Three or more tones sounded at the same time (page 122)
chorus/choir	A group of singers (page 102)
composed song	Music written by one or more persons (page 196)
composer	A person who writes music
conductor	A person who directs a group of musicians
diction	Pronouncing words correctly and clearly when speaking or singing (page 39)
downbeat	The first beat of a measure, often stressed
downward	Melodic direction toward lower sounding pitches
duple	Set of two (pages 62, 322)
duple meter	Meter based on macrobeats that travel in groups of two
dynamics	One of the ways to make music expressive, these are the levels of loud and soft in a musical work (page 181)
echo	The exact imitation of a given phrase, sound, or pattern
expressive	A way of performing music that shows mood or feeling (page 31)
fast	Quick
folk song	A song passed down from generation to generation that most people learn by hearing others sing it
form	The way a musical composition is organized
forte (f)	A mark in music that tells musicians to perform at a loud or strong dynamic level
high	A sound that is in the upper range or register of an instrument or voice

improvise	To create and perform music, speech, or movement on the spot (page 80)
interlude	A short musical passage that is sometimes used to connect larger sections of music
interval	The distance between two pitches (page 127)
leading tone	The tone that leads upward to the home tone; the solfège note "ti" in a major scale
long tone	A tone that is not short and that sounds for a long time
loud	Not quiet
low	A sound that is in the bottom range or register of an instrument or voice
lullaby	Quiet music that is usually used to rock a baby to sleep
macrobeat	The steady beat or heartbeat of the music; the basic beat in a rhythm pattern
mallet	A special stick with a round ball on one end used to play a percussion instrument
march	Music with a strong steady beat for moving
measure	In musical notation, a group of beats separated by bar lines (page 60)
melodic direction	The upward, downward, or repeated movement of tones in melodies
melodic rhythm	The pattern of sounds and silences in a melody; in songs, this is often the same as the rhythm of the words
melody	A series of pitches that create the tune of a piece of music
meter	The repeated pattern of beats per measure (page 60)
microbeat	The even division of the macrobeat
mood	The way a composer, artist, or writer wants you to feel when you hear the music, see the art, or read the book or story (page 138)
music criteria	Standards by which music and performance are evaluated (page 211)
orchestra	A large group of musicians playing string, brass, woodwind, and percussion instruments
ostinato	A short musical pattern (melodic or rhythmic) that is repeated throughout all or part of a musical work (page 19)
patriotic music	Music that helps us express our love for our country (page 32)
pattern	A series of pitches, sounds, silences, or musical forms that repeat
pentatonic	Any five-tone scale ("do," "re," "mi," "sol," "la") or music that is based on that five-tone scale
phrase	A musical thought or idea
piano (p)	A mark in music that tells musicians to perform at a soft or quiet dynamic level
piano	A keyboard instrument that sounds when the keys are pressed by the fingers, which makes a hammer strike a string that is tuned to a specific pitch
pitch	A specific musical tone
pitched	A type of musical instrument that can produce specific musical tones and can be used to play melodies
pizzicato	To play a string instrument by plucking the string rather than using the bow (page 124)
refrain	In a song, a section of music, sung or played, that is repeated between verses
repeated pattern	A pattern that occurs more than once (page 18)

repeated tones	Tones that are the same and occur more than once (page 12)
resonate	To sound through vibration
rest	A symbol that indicates a silent unit of time
rhythm	The pattern of sounds and silences in music (the duration or length of time notes are sounded) (page 181)
rhythm of the words	The pattern of sounds and silences in the words to a song or poem; in songs, this is often the same as the melodic rhythm
rondo	A musical form in which the first section is repeated several times with a different section in between, such as ABACA and ABACADA (pages 157, 171)
setting	The time (when), place (where), and action (who or what) in which music, art, or a story occurs or develops (page 182)
short tone	A tone that is not long and sounds only a brief time
singing voice	The voice we use to share melodies and songs
skip	The distance from one tone to a tone that is more than a step away from it (up or down) (page 12)
slow	Not quick; unhurried
soft	Quiet
solo	A performance by one person (page 173)
sound source	The instrument or device making a sound; the origin of sound (page 207)
speaking voice	The voice we use to say words and make other sounds that are not melodies or songs
steady beat	The even pulse of music; the heartbeat or macrobeat of music (pages 15, 56)
step	The distance from one tone to the tone next to it (up or down) (page 12)
style	The special way something is done, created, or performed (page 177)
syncopation	An unexpected change from the normal rhythm or meter, or the emphasis not on the beat
tempo	The speed of the beat; the speed of music (page 181)
texture	The quality of a musical work that is determined by the number and types of its voices, instruments, melodies, and harmonies (page 197)
theme music	Music that is familiar because it is identified with a character, movie, TV show, or radio program
tie	A curved line connecting or tying together two notes of the same pitch so they are played as if they were one note
tone	The sound of a specific musical pitch
tone color	The sound that is special or unique to a voice or an instrument
triple	Set of three (pages 63, 322)
triple meter	Meter based on macrobeats that travel in groups of three
unpitched	Types of musical instruments (mostly percussion) that do not produce a specific tone and cannot play a melody

upbeat	The last beat of a measure, leading to the downbeat
upward	Melodic direction toward higher sounding pitches
verse	In a song, the sections of music with the same melody but different words each time, and usually separated by a refrain

Instruments

banjo	A folk instrument related to the guitar, with a fretted fingerboard, long neck, a circular body, and four or five strings (pages 180, 217)
bell	A hollow metal percussion instrument that is sounded by a clapper inside (hanging or loose) or a striker outside
bow	A tool like a long stick made of wood and horsehair, drawn across the strings of a string instrument to make the sound
cello	The tenor voice and second largest member of the string family, whose range falls between that of the viola and the double bass, played by resting the instrument between the knees while seated, and plucking or bowing the strings (page 212)
cymbals	A metal percussion instrument made of two round plates, held by straps, and sounded by striking them together
dàn bâu	A single-string instrument from Vietnam made of wood or bamboo, played by plucking the string and pulling the spout, or wammy bar, forward and back to change the pitch (page 251)
double bass/string bass	The bass voice and lowest range in the string family, this is the largest string instrument and is often played standing up either by plucking or bowing the strings (page 208)
drum	A percussion instrument made of a hollow shell or cylinder with a drumhead (plastic or skin) stretched over one or both ends that sounds when struck with the hands, sticks, wire brushes, or mallets
fiddle	A name used for the violin when performing folk music (pages 180, 217)
glockenspiel	A melodic percussion instrument with a high range, consisting of thin metal bars (often shiny steel) that sound when struck by mallets
guitar	A plucked or strummed string instrument used often by folk and rock musicians, with six or more strings, frets (usually 19), a shape something between a pear and a figure eight, and a round sound hole (page 217)
hammered dulcimer	A folk instrument with many strings attached to a wooden box and played by striking the strings with little hammers (page 180)
jingle bells	A metal percussion instruments made of a set of bells attached together that sound when shaken

koto	A Japanese musical instrument, six feet long, consisting of 13 strings stretched over 13 bridges on an oblong wooden box, and played by three tsume (claws) on the fingers that pluck the strings (pages 251, 254, 261)
metal	A type of percussion instrument whose sound is made by the striking together of metal parts
metallophone	A melodic percussion instrument made of metal bars attached to a wooden box that sound when struck by mallets
pipa	A Chinese lute (a musical instrument like a guitar) made of wood with bamboo frets, played by plucking the four strings (page 251)
rhythm sticks	A wood percussion instrument that is sounded by scraping or striking one upon the other or on another surface
sitar	A Middle Eastern string instrument with a long neck, 20 movable frets to produce a wide variety of modes and tunings, and originally having three strings (modern sitars usually have 17 strings), which are plucked to make the sound (page 250)
skins	A type of percussion instrument whose sound is made by striking (with a special stick or the hands) a sheet of skin or plastic that has been stretched over the end of a hollow shell or cylinder
viola	The alto voice and second highest pitched member of the string family, lower in pitch than the violin and higher in pitch than the cello, played by holding the instrument under the chin and either plucking or bowing the strings (page 220)
violin	The soprano voice and highest pitched member of the string family, played by holding the instrument under the chin and either plucking or bowing the strings (pages 202–203)
Welsh harp	A wooden many-string instrument from Wales, usually about six feet tall and wooden in the shape of a triangle, played while sitting and plucking the strings with the fingers (page 250)
wood	A type of percussion instrument whose sound is made by the striking together of wooden parts
woodblock	A percussion instrument whose sound is made by striking a block of hollow wood with a wooden mallet or striker
xylophone	A melodic percussion instrument made of wooden bars that sound when struck by mallets

Symbols

	bar line	A line that goes from the bottom to the top of a staff and divides the staff into measures
	double bar line	Two bar lines placed at the end of a staff to point out the end of a section or composition
	fermata	A symbol that means to hold or pause (all parts), or stretch the sound longer than it normally would be heard or performed
	line note	A written note with a staff line through its center
	repeat sign	Two dots in the second and third spaces in front of a double bar line telling you to play or sing the section of music over again from the beginning. A forward repeat sign has two dots after the double bar line and tells you to repeat only from that point on.
	space note	A note written between the lines on a staff

Notes and Rests

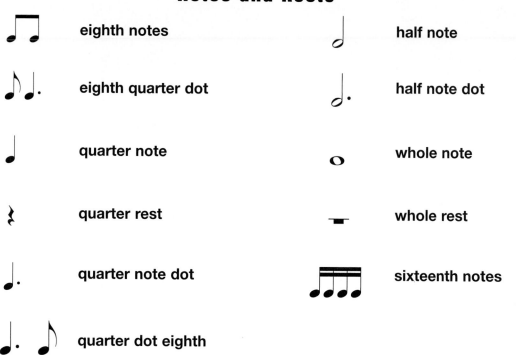

eighth notes		**half note**	
eighth quarter dot		**half note dot**	
quarter note		**whole note**	
quarter rest		**whole rest**	
quarter note dot		**sixteenth notes**	
quarter dot eighth			

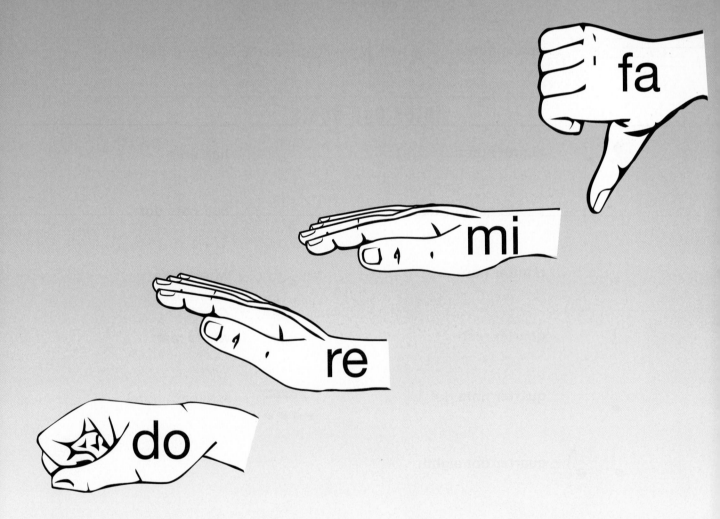

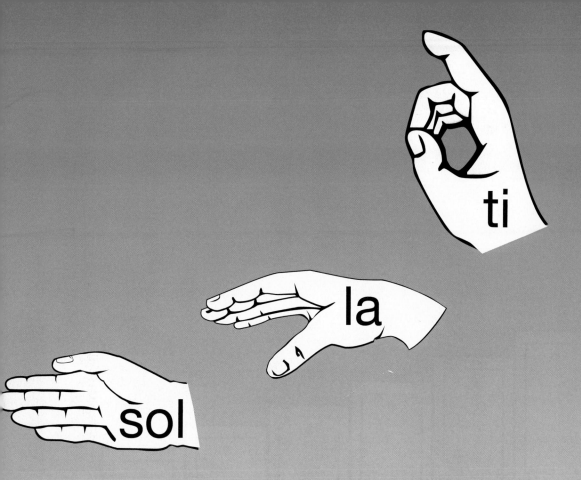

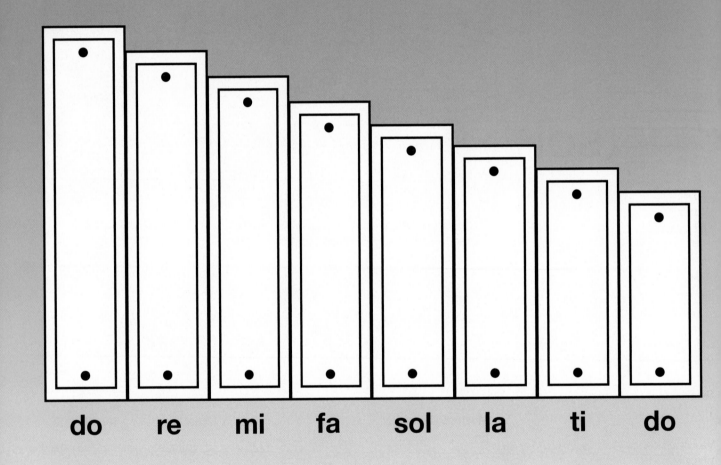

Index

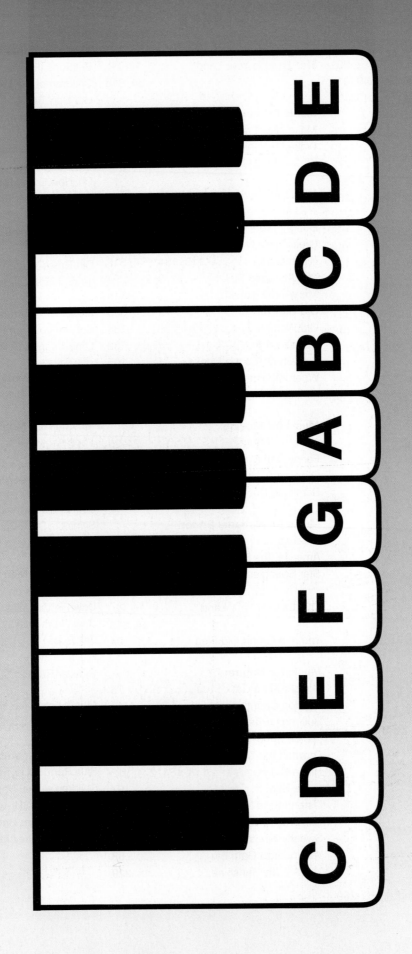